I04E4065

TIME MANAGEMENT FOR STUDENTS

TIME MANAGEMENT FOR STUDENTS

THE INTERNATIONAL EDITION

SUDHIR PANSE

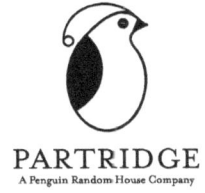

PARTRIDGE

A Penguin Random House Company

Copyright © 2014 by Sudhir Panse.

ISBN:	Hardcover	978-1-4828-3360-7
	Softcover	978-1-4828-3361-4
	eBook	978-1-4828-3359-1

All rights reserved. No part of this book may be used or reproduced by any means, graphic, electronic, or mechanical, including photocopying, recording, taping or by any information storage retrieval system without the written permission of the publisher except in the case of brief quotations embodied in critical articles and reviews.

Because of the dynamic nature of the Internet, any web addresses or links contained in this book may have changed since publication and may no longer be valid. The views expressed in this work are solely those of the author and do not necessarily reflect the views of the publisher, and the publisher hereby disclaims any responsibility for them.

To order additional copies of this book, contact
Partridge India
000 800 10062 62
orders.india@partridgepublishing.com

www.partridgepublishing.com/india

Contents

Preface

B efore we start, a few words on how I came to write this book.

All my life I have been fortunate to belong to the most fulfilling of all professions—teaching. I started out as a junior lecturer in the physics department of a college in Mumbai and in course of time rose to become its Principal, and subsequently the Chief Academic Officer (Director B.C.U.D.) of the university of Mumbai. Besides teaching, I carried out and supervised research in physics and 'physics education' at the university of Mumbai, YCMOU, and some other leading institutions in the city. I was always keen to widen the ambit of my teaching experience. I worked as 'Teacher-In-Charge' for 'National Service Scheme' (N.S.S.) in the college, and organized Social Service camps for my students in remote villages of Maharashtra. I also worked as the 'Chief Coordinator' of the Study Centre of 'Indira Gandhi National Open University' (IGNOU) in the College, where army personnel and other adults working in different jobs and professions enrolled as part time students. I was also closely associated for many years with the 'Homi Bhabha Study Circle' conducted at 'Homi Bhabha Centre for Science Education', Mumbai for meritorious undergraduates in science.

This long and varied experience involved continual interaction with students of different age groups, levels and backgrounds. Not infrequently did I share their personal optimism and despair, joy and sorrow. I observed and analyzed the factors underlying their performance and how, when and why it improved or declined. I could, of course, discern the well-known factors such as socio-economic, cultural and family background as well as personal motivation and drive that lay behind their success. But I saw in due course that there was one more equally critical factor that was perhaps not widely appreciated. It is the ability to manage time effectively. What is more, I came to the crucial insight that while the other factors were complex and largely beyond the student's control, the ability to manage time can be acquired relatively easily, provided we understand the basic points regarding time management and practice it aided by practical and convenient ways. This realization led me to write this book.

Acknowledgements

I wish to record my gratitude to all the teacher colleagues and students with whom I shared my thoughts over the years about this subject and whose valuable feedback helped me shape my ideas and insights on time management elaborated on in this book.

In addition, mention must be made of two of my friends. Dr. Arvind Kumar, former Director of 'Homi Bhabha Center for Science Education' was kind enough to critically go through the manuscript and make valuable suggestions. Professor J. B. Joshi, former Director of 'Institute of Chemical Technology, Mumbai' and presently 'Homi Bhabha Chair' Professor at Bhabha Atomic Research Centre (BARC) can be described as an idol of practicing Time Management. Discussions with him on this and many other topics were very illuminating. I sincerely thank both of them.

Sudhir Panse.

1

Why You Should Read This Book.

This book is written with a single clear purpose in mind. It is that our students should master the technique of time management.

Two legitimate questions can (and should) arise. 'Why time management?' and 'Why students?'

Well, the second question first!

Why students?

Is it because elders already know it?

No! Absolutely no! Not at all!

Few elders know these techniques; and very few out of those few practice them!

But we want to specifically talk to you, dear students! This is because you are in your formative years. You can learn new techniques quickly. You can adopt different patterns of behavior easily, and thereby can reap maximum benefit for yourselves.

But, that is not all. There is one more reason; and that is more important. And also, that is the answer to the first question, "Why time management?"

Today's youngsters need the technique of Time Management, more than their parents. Today's generation needs Time Management far more acutely, than what the earlier generations needed.

Why? Because, your world today is more challenging than the world of yester years. The generation today faces many stiff challenges, and also has many exciting opportunities. Those, who succeed in bringing out their inner talents and managing their time efficiently, will fetch tremendous rewards; those who fail to do so, will face serious disappointments. Today's world is very competitive; and also the competition is at a different level, from that faced by earlier generations. The competition you face now is indirectly, and the one which you will face tomorrow will be directly, at the global level. No longer is your competition restricted to the boy or girl next door; or the one in your school or college. You are all actually competing with the unknown intelligent, hardworking youngsters growing up in China, U.S.A., Europe and elsewhere.

Also, the technology today has opened up so many vistas, that the expectations from life have increased manifold. There is enormous peer pressure. You have to score good marks in the examination! Yes, and also you must exercise and maintain good physique! Yes, and also you must be smart and should know all details of Bollywood and Hollywood gossip! Yes, and also you must show excellence in some art or sports, preferably both!.......... And the list can go on! In short, you should achieve in real life, what a hero of a typical Hindi movie does on the screen! At least many of you aspire to do so.

But, leave aside the heroes of Hindi movies. There are young boys and girls around you in real life, who actually do achieve many of these things. Perhaps you have wondered many times, how do they do it?

How do they manage to achieve success in so many diverse fields simultaneously? You, perhaps, think that these children are born with some extra talent, or that, they are simply lucky—'the God's favored ones'. You, then, conclude that you are not so lucky; and that is not your fault.

Well! You are right and you are wrong. Actually, you are partially right; and you are completely wrong!

You are wrong because such boys and girls are not born with any exceptional talent, nor are they God's more favored children. But, you are right, they are lucky.

Lucky in what way? They are lucky because they have stumbled upon the techniques of time management, mostly by accident. Actually, all of us do stumble upon these fortunate accidents in our lives; but most of us miss their significance; and lose golden opportunities.

But now, this book will make a difference!

Now, no longer need you wait for such lucky accidents to occur. The techniques for time management especially for students are explained here comprehensively and systematically for the first time. This book is not a general discussion on the importance of time management. There are specific tips given here which can be followed easily. This book is written such that you can assimilate the matter quickly and *practice it.*

'Practice it' are the key words.

This is *not* a book, which is to be read once and tossed aside.

This is *not* a book, which is to be learnt by heart as preparation of an examination.

This is *not* a story book or, a book for casual reading.

This is *not* a text book either. Nor is this a guide to any subject in your school or college examination.

But this book will change your life, as no other book will!

This is a 'work book'.

Read it at least twice initially.

Then keep on going through it regularly. For best results, do so at least once every month.

Also, note that this book is written and presented in a different format.

There are no long paragraphs, no lengthy descriptions. The writing is sharp and crisp, and the style deliberately conversational.

You only see concise, focused sentences written in steps.

That makes it easier and faster to go through this book. You see, a book on 'Time Management' must be written, so that there is effective time management in reading the book itself!

And, we repeat (because this important point needs repetition), this is not a book to be read once and tossed away. Read it frequently and you will reap immense benefits.

And yes! We must point out to you. Now, that you are reading this book, you are indeed lucky!

Very soon you will learn and practice the most effective techniques for a successful life, the techniques of Time Management.

Congratulations; and all the best!

2

A Note for the Parents.

Dear Parents!

At the outset let us congratulate you for being a very responsible parent. You have done a wonderful job for your child. It is a universal fact that all parents love their children. They give them gifts. They arrange for their best education. They make thoughtful financial investments for securing their future. All this is common. The more enlightened of them spend time and money, and take efforts to ensure that their children possess good qualities, and develop an enriched and wholesome personality.

But, what you have done today is definitely of vital significance. You have handed over a master key of success in life to your child. That is quite special. Your child, of course, loves you; and would definitely remember all the things you have done for him/her; but this one deed of yours would be remembered and appreciated by him/her for years to come.

You will also feel proud of yourself and your child, because of his/her achievements, once he/she masters the technique of time management.

But gifting the book to your child is not enough, because this is a 'work book'. It is to be followed. It is to be practiced. The tips given here are to be applied by your child in his/her daily routine. Only then will the benefits be reaped by your child. For this purpose, your help, intervention, monitoring may be required. Let the project of 'Mastering the Techniques of Time Management' become a joint project of both, you and your child.

But, a word of caution! Remember, your role is just that of a facilitator, a guide. The actual decisions are to be taken by your child, and those decisions are to be put into actions by your child. Be very careful about this strategy. Do not make your child dependent upon you for practicing Time Management.

For example, a key factor in time management, as you will come to know as you read further, is preparing a 'to do' list every day. You can ensure that he/she prepares the list every day without fail. Also, you can discuss about what activities should be included in the list. (Make the list as exhaustive as possible.) But the final decision about activities will be that of the child. The job of actually writing down the list would be that of the child.

A similar caution should be executed for other activities also. The main idea is that, when the project is complete, time management should become a habit, a natural behavioral pattern of your child. The child should become confident that he/she can manage independently. Ideally, your role should be confined to the initial period of six months to one year. After that period, it should fade away.

You are successful in your mission, if your role becomes redundant after one year!

We wish you all the best.

3

The Meaning of Time Management

A company manager manages the company.

Your mother (or, in general the lady of the house) manages the home.

Your teacher manages the class.

Is 'Time Management' the same as management of a company, or of a home or of a class?

No. By no means.

In the earlier examples, the word 'management' means managing affairs related to the company, or the daily chores related to home or the activities of students in the class.

But no one can manage or control anything related with the flow of time.

Time flows uniformly, independent of effect of any external factor. The Sun rises after every 24 hours and a new day dawns. The Earth moves round the Sun with its standard speed, and a year is over after 365 days. No one can do anything that would alter this flow of time.

Yes, there is the Theory of Relativity of Einstein, which shows that the flow of Time for an observer is affected by his relative velocity and his acceleration. But that happens significantly only in very special circumstances and it is irrelevant for affecting the flow of time in our lives.

Nor can we store time in a safe to manage it; or put it in a bank as a 'fixed deposit', and withdraw it and use it whenever needed!

We cannot think of constructing a dam to create a huge reservoir of time, so that it can be directed to the areas and people who need it badly!

No, nothing can be done to alter, affect, and manage the flow of time! And yet it is possible to practice time management successfully.

This is an essential point that you must understand clearly. *We cannot manage the flow of time, but we can practice time management.*

How is it possible?

Well! That precisely is the secret, and that is what this book is about. A basic and important point in this respect is that the techniques of time management are very simple. In fact, they are so simple, that their simplicity itself may deceive you. But, more on this later.

A good beginning is to consider the question: 'what is *not* Time Management?'

You, perhaps, think that Time Management means being workaholic.——Wrong!

You, perhaps, think that Time Management means continuously being busy with work or studies.————Wrong!

You, perhaps, think that Time Management means spending very little or no time for entertainment or sports.————Wrong again!

You, perhaps, think that time management for students means 'wasting' no time in watching TV and 'using' all the time for studies.—————Wrong again!

These are flawed conceptions of Time Management.

Indeed, Time Management means just the opposite.

It means doing all the other things that interest you along with your work and studies; and excelling in everything.

It means finding time for TV, for sports and for entertainment, without losing on studies and work.

We will tell you how you can get time for all the things you want to do. We will tell you how you can study faster and better. We will tell you how you can get rid of exam tension. By using the techniques of Time Management, you can achieve in one year, what you could not have dreamt of achieving in two years or more. And this would be true for every year to come in your life! That is, with Time Management your achievements and enjoyments in one life would be at least equivalent to those in two lives!

Also important is the fact that you are at present in the student phase of your life.

This is the phase, in which your personality is molded, and habits are formed.

Also, this is the phase in which you can easily judge your progress and measure the level of success achieved. (It is not always easy to do so in your later life, when the meanings of the words 'progress' and 'success' acquire complex dimensions.) The criterion simply is excellence in performance in examinations along with excellence in extracurricular activities in chosen fields (such as, sport or singing or dancing or painting or any such other activity).

In short, by learning time management in your student days, you are laying the foundation for an enriched and successful life.

Also, do not expect instant miracles. Techniques of time management are simple, and definitely give positive results from the beginning; but the real advantages are seen only when they are practiced consistently for a few months. And after a year or so, you will notice that you have surpassed many of your classmates (some of whom you might have thought were more intelligent than you). You will find yourself among the front runners.

4

The First Step: Know Thyself

The first step in time management is to examine and analyze how you spend your time every day. What are your activities every day? What is their sequence? How much time do you spend for each activity? Try and answer these questions, and record your answers. Be as specific as possible.

Suppose you:

Get up in the morning at 6 O' clock.

Come out of bed at 6.05.

Brush your teeth for 5 minutes (6.10).

Have your morning tea or coffee for 10 minutes (6.20).

Go to toilet and take bath (20 minutes, 6.40).

Comb your hair and dress up for going to school or class (10 minutes, 6.50).

Have your breakfast and a glass of milk (10 minutes, 7.00).

Put on your shoes (2 minutes, 7.02).

Leave for the school or class (7.05).

Say, you take 10 minutes to reach there (7.15).

The above schedule is just one example. (And it is only for a part of the day.) Obviously, it may not be the same for every student.

But the point to note is the way it is recorded.

Don't just say, 'it takes about an hour for me to get ready in the morning and leave for the school'. That is too broad a statement. It gives no information, which will help time management.

So, be specific and bring in as many details as possible. Also, don't just 'think' how much time you feel you might be taking for every activity.

Actually look the time in the clock and record it.

'Record it' are the key words. You have to *write down* the timings in a diary.

You might think, 'how can I do that? I am in such a hurry to leave for the school (or class) at that time; not a single minute to spare! How can I take out time for writing down time?' And you are quite right.

But you must do it!

How? How will you take this first step in learning time management? How can you rush through your morning chores and also record the time required for each different activity?

Well, you can do it in two ways.

One way is to have someone in your family help you. You can perhaps ask your mother or father, or may be your grandmother or grandfather to help you. (No doubt, people in your family will be quite willing to help you in this project. Also, you will need this help only for one week, because this exercise is to be done only for one week.)

Let him or her record the observations in a diary for you.

Remember, this (recording of the present time schedule) is not an activity that will go on and on. Do it only for one week.

But do it on all days of the week regularly and sincerely.

The second way is of self dependence, and it is also not very difficult.

You know the sequence of your activities in the morning, for example.

Jot down the sequence in a diary. Then all that you have to do is to look at the clock and note the starting and end time of any activity. This should not be difficult.

The key word in the above sentences is *diary.*

You have to record the information in a diary. Do not use loose sheets to record the data.

It might surprise you, but a diary is the most important tool for time management.

This sentence is very important. So, we repeat it.

The diary is the most important tool for time management.

Actually, time is such a potent entity, flowing uniformly and autonomously without reference to anything external. Nothing can influence its course, yet it affects everything and everybody.

And a diary is such a small, non- descript entity! It hardly costs anything, or hardly occupies any space. It involves no big technology.

But make no mistake about it.

The habit of using a diary will make a big change in your life.

And that change will be for the better.

This habit will virtually bring about a revolution in your life, the importance of which you will realize in the years to come.

You see, it does happen often that big and spectacular events that bring about revolutionary changes, crucially depend on a tiny, non-descript tool.

You, of course, know the long sea voyages of brave navigators from Europe in the eighteenth century, don't you?

The voyages became possible and successful, only because of a tiny and simple device they carried on their ships.

It was so tiny, that it occupied negligible space on their ships, which otherwise were loaded with huge quantities of food and drinking water and ammunition and what not! No doubt, all those things were necessary.

But what made the voyages possible and successful, was a small compass needle, sitting on the desk of the captain and ensuring all the time that the ship was moving in the proper direction.

If the compass needle were not there, Vasco de Gamma might never have reached India, and Columbus might never have discovered America. What is more important, they would not have been able to chart their paths for other ships to follow later on to the same destinations!

The era of European dominance over other continents would not have dawned.

Such is the importance of a small compass needle in the world history.

Similar is the importance of diary in your life.

In your school bag and on your study table, there are many things. There are books and note-books and a compass box and a pencil box and a set of pens, and so on! These are, no doubt, essential for your studies.

Every year, every teacher tells you in the beginning of the year, what books and note-books you must purchase for studying. And your parents ensure that you have got all those things.

But, no one possibly tells you to purchase a diary every year and to use it. At least no one would insist on that.

But we are insisting on that.

We are emphasizing that.

The diary is a very small item. And it is hardly costly.

But, it plays the same role played by a compass needle on a ship leaving for a long voyage on the sea.

You see, your life is also a long voyage that you are about to undertake.

You want to be successful. Your parents want you to be successful.

For that, they ensure that you are equipped with all the necessary things you need. This is precisely the purpose of the student phase of your life.

In this phase, you should get all the knowledge and information and acquire all the skills and techniques that are needed in this voyage, called 'life'.

But there is one more tool that you definitely need.

It is the tool that ensures that the direction of your voyage is right, that you are charting out the right course, and that your schedule is perfect.

This simple tool is the *diary*!

Just as a compass needle ensures that the ship is always on the right track and would reach the destination, as planned; the diary would ensure that you are always on the right track and at the right time throughout your life.

What type of a diary can you use?

Well! We are going to tell you to use the diary for two purposes.

One purpose is to write your long term and short term plans; and the other purpose is to record important developments and happenings on a daily basis.

The diary should be such that there is one page for one day.

There are some diaries, where a day on a page is further subdivided into hours. Such diaries are useful for executives and managers. You can use them in your later life.

But, in your student days, it is preferable that you use simple diaries having one page for one day.

Further, our academic year is from June to April; and normally most of the easily available diaries in the market are from Jan to Dec. The two do not match. Also, it is not necessary that you start using the diary, and learn the technique of time management from the beginning of a new academic year. You don't need to wait for that. Start it on an auspicious day.

And that auspicious day is *TODAY*.

Have a diary, and start using it today, whatever may be the month and date!

So, simply purchase a blank diary with no dates of about 200 pages, and put the dates, devoting one page for one day. (Use the next diary after 200 days.)

The size of this diary should preferably be about 12 cm x 18.5 cm.

We are giving these detailed instructions, because a diary is such an important tool in time management.

Purchasing a proper diary is important, but what is more important is to develop a habit of using the diary.

All successful people regularly maintain diaries.

You might think that they have to do so because they are successful and are holding high positions. You might be saying to yourself, 'I am not a big person, nor am I holding any high position. My day is not filled with appointments with different people, or for meetings at different places. I am simply a student, and most of my days are routine. Why should I maintain a diary? I will do so, when I become big and important and busy'.

Well, the truth is exactly the opposite.

Not that successful people maintain diaries, because they are successful and are holding high positions.

They are successful and are holding high positions, because they maintain diaries!

But more about it later.

So, the first important point which we want to emphasize is that you must have a diary, a good diary, and you must cultivate a habit of using it daily.

There is one more point.

Electronic diaries are also available these days. Mobile phones also have features of a diary. Computers can work as diaries. These electronic diaries have some advantages; but actually, they are not a substitute for a diary of about 200 pages. Such a diary has one important distinguishing feature: it is just a diary, and nothing else. A mobile phone or a computer can do many other jobs also. We strongly advise you not to use an electronic diary during your student days, when you are learning the technique of time management, and developing the habit of maintaining a diary.

You can, and should, use electronic devices in your later life with their associated advantages. But for the present, get a simple diary; *and use it regularly.*

So, what is the 'step one' for time management?

Have a good diary, and start using it.

And how do you start using it?

Record your daily activities from the time you get out of bed in the morning to the time you go to bed at night and note the actual time taken for each of the activities.

Be as specific as possible and put as many details as possible.

Do this consistently every day for one full week.

Some of you may think that this is ridiculously simple, how can it help me? But this is not true.

You will soon notice that it is easy, but not trivial to record the *actual* time that you take for every activity.

And even if you find it simple and trivial, do it none the less for one week; and do it sincerely.

This exercise will help you know yourself, understand yourself better. And the starting point of any self improvement program is precisely this: 'know thyself!' Because you can improve only that, which you have understood well.

One more point.

As you begin, some of you may quickly see possibilities of saving time in the daily routine, and start working on them.

But do not try any such thing in the first week. No need to rush through the program.

Just collect the basic data about yourself. That is enough for the first week. Analysis and improvements will follow later.

5

The Rule of 10%

What is the purpose of the project of 'Know Thyself'? What is the purpose of recording your daily activities; and the time required for each activity?

Obviously, it is to identify the possibilities where time can be saved, and to explore areas where daily routine can be done faster and better.

This is not difficult. You can save time, and you can do things faster and better, and you can do it very easily.

For this, you must first understand the 'Rule of 10%'. What is this rule?

Well! The 'Rule of 10%' simply states that, *'in any area of human activity an improvement of 10% is always easily possible'.*

Understand what the rule says. Actually, it tells two things. The first thing is that there is always a scope for improvement in any human activity. It does not talk about any specific type of activity. It does not say, 'the activity with unsatisfactory results'. It does not say 'the activity, which needs improvement'. It only says that it is possible to improve any human activity.

This is because scope of improvement reduces to zero, only if a thing has already attained perfection. No change can make that thing better, which is already perfect.

But no human being is perfect; and hence no human activity is perfect. Therefore, there is always a scope of improvement in any human activity.

The second thing the rule states is about how much improvement is easily possible. You see, to reach ideal condition and to reach perfection, many possible changes can be worked out logically. But human behavior is not governed by logic. It is governed by emotions, and by habits formed over years. There is a psychological resistance to any change. So, a change in human activity is not easy. What the rule says further, therefore, is that you can aim at a 10% change, a 10% improvement. That is an easily achievable target.

So, try to make a 10% improvement. Try to see how you can save 10% of time that you spend on any activity. Don't be over ambitious. Don't be over enthusiastic. Your target initially is just 10%, not more.

A little reflection will show you that this is not difficult.

For example, if you take 60 minutes to prepare yourself in the morning for going to school, reduce that time just by 6 minutes. That should not be difficult.

If you are taking 20 minutes to reach the school, make it 18 minutes. That should not be difficult.

If you sleep for 8 hours at night, reduce that time by 45 minutes or so. That should be possible.

So, just start developing a habit that you do all things (or, at least as many out of them as possible) 10% faster. Just 10%!

You may start wondering, what is the use of saving 5 minutes in the morning, 2 minutes while reaching the school and 10 minutes in some other activity.

You might be expecting us to suggest you that how one hour a day can be saved, if you reduce that much time from your time of watching TV. Then there is a clear slot of 1 hour duration, which can be devoted to study. But we are telling you to save a few minutes here and a few minutes there! You are justified in asking us, what is the use of such distributed intervals of time?

Well, Yes! We will tell you how to save hours also, and put them to productive use. But please understand that such possibilities are rare.

You, of course know '50-50' one day cricket matches. Some batsmen there score huge totals at an unbelievably fast rate. How do they do it? Not by continuously hitting boundaries and sixes! If you analyze the statistics carefully, you will find that not even 30% of the runs are scored in boundaries and sixes. seventy percent or more runs come from singles and doubles. And the real skill of scoring runs fast comes from converting singles into doubles. That requires a special training of running between the wickets.

The boundaries and sixes are spectacular and attract applause from the spectators. But the real foundation of large score at fast rate lies in converting singles into doubles.

The same is true in your life. It would be a folly to think that you can reduce time of sleep by 2 hours, and time for watching TV by 1 hour and will have enough time to study or to do other work. Also, don't fool yourself by thinking, that with a strong determination you can be successful in implementing and maintaining such drastic cuts in your sleep and TV time. That can be done rarely but is not desirable, in general. (In any case you must have almost 7 hours sleep every day.)

So, understand the power of the rule of 10%. While doing this, you are not doing anything spectacular. You are not rushing through the things. You don't have a feeling of being harassed. But you do have a positive and lasting advantage.

Pure arithmetic will tell you that by implementing the rule of 10%, you will get nearly two and half hours per day! This means in one year you will get more than 30 extra days or more than one extra month! That is a huge, huge time!

Of course, life is not pure arithmetic. But, actually even if you get an hour and a half extra every day, it will make a big difference to your life.

The question, which may come to your mind (or, actually, which *should* come to your mind!) is that, this extra time is fragmented as 5 minutes here and 2 minutes there and so on. What is the use of this time?

Well! One reason, why we want you to increase your speed of completing things by 10% is because we want you to develop that habit. Doing things a little faster than your normal speed is always possible, and helpful. If you develop this habit right from your student days, it will benefit you throughout your life. No need to make undue haste; but always be quick in completing the work at hand.

And don't underestimate the importance of minutes. Even a few extra minutes available can be put to a very fruitful use.

Actually, this is what this book is about. How to get extra time and how to spend extra time! This we will be discussing as we proceed. But here we will give some tips.

Let us say, for example, that you save 5 minutes in the morning before leaving for the school. You can use this time to have a morning prayer every day before starting your day (to whichever God you believe in), or just sit quietly for 5 minutes and do positive thinking. (Later on there is a chapter on 'Power of Positive Thinking').

Alternatively, you can glance through the morning news paper before leaving and may get a quick update on sports (or on Bollywood gossip!) as well as headlines. If you can do that every day, you will soon find that you can impress your friends and teachers by being up to date in general knowledge.

The point is, there are always ways and means to utilize the extra time that you get. You have to think a little bit and be imaginative about it, and include it in your planning of the day.

Actually, do you know something? A time interval of five or ten minutes is not at all insignificant. In fact, it is a substantial time! Really! But we fail to understand this, because we spend a large part of our time neither for doing any useful activity, nor for any enjoyment. We spend (or, in fact, *waste*) a large amount of time as 'switch over time'.

Now, what is a 'switch over time'? Well! It is the time between ending any one activity and starting any new activity. There is this 'in-between time gap' for most of us, which is just natural. We are not particularly doing anything during that time interval. That time is the 'switch over time'. Try and minimize that time as much as possible.

There is one thing common among all successful people, whatever may be their fields of success. They very quickly switch over from one activity to another. They do not require any time between closing one activity and starting any new activity. And then they instantly immerse themselves in their new activity. They have trained their brains, and their minds to instantly get focused on the new activity at hand. It is like closing one book and opening another. Better still, it is like changing a TV channel, using the remote control. Within a fraction of a second the TV screen, which was showing a cricket match until then, starts showing a movie! And this happens without any interruption, without any time lag.

That is, perhaps, the ideal condition. But we are not a machine. We are not an electronic gadget. We are human beings. We cannot function like a TV. Agreed!

But many of us have a problem that can be termed as 'starting trouble'. We think internally, 'Oh! I have just completed one activity. Now I am going to start another activity. But there I must have a gap of few minutes.' The 'few minutes' then become 'some more minutes', and then 'ten minutes' and then 'fifteen minutes' and so on. Considering the fact that you have to switch on from one activity to another so frequently in a day, the total time wasted in this way becomes a significant part of your day.

Again, we are not saying that you must rush through the activities. It may be natural to take a few minutes while starting a new activity. But ideally that time should be two minutes. May be, it can be up to five minutes. But quite often it extends beyond that. And that is not acceptable. That must be avoided.

Particularly, one must try and develop this habit in student days. Not only will it make a big difference now to your performance as a student, but it will also lead to success and happiness in your later life.

Initially, whenever you switch over from one activity to another, you can say to yourself, 'Quick! I make a quick shift!' Just say this! But this is not just a sentence. This is a mantra for mastering time management. Repeat it every day, every time you make a switch over. Do this for a year, and it will become a habit. It will become a part of your personality. It will remain with you for your entire life and will give you rich dividends.

But the second point in this respect is more important. We often tend to do things slowly, because we do not know what to do with the available time. This is true in case of many elders also.

Do you know 'work' is a stretchable thing, like rubber? Do you know that work expands to fill the available time? Yes, it is true! This is one of the famous Parkinson's laws of management. 'Work expands to fill the available time.' Many people quite often keep on prolonging the work at hand; simply because they do not know what next to do with the time after the work at hand is over. Not that any one does it consciously. But this does happen subconsciously; especially when one does not know how to fill the time with more and more meaningful activities. Gradually, this becomes a habit. Lingering at the job at hand becomes a routine. Such people tend to prolong every bit of work. Then they complain that there is too much work for them. They complain that there is no time for them to do anything extra!

It is also said that 'a busy man always gets time' This is because, a busy man (or woman) knows how to complete work faster and better, and use the extra time available for other productive work, or for fun and enjoyment.

Also, you are in the student phase of your life. Your main objective in this phase is to learn skills and form good habits to prepare yourself for achieving success in your later life. Any other benefits at this stage are secondary. For example, when your teacher tells you to write an essay, it is obviously not expected that you will necessarily become a writer in your later life. But the intention is that you should develop the capacity of forming and expressing your views on any given topic, because that will definitely help you in your later life. That is the idea.

Or, may be, some of you have joined classes to learn drawing; or vocal music. Or, may be, some of you play cricket, or basket ball, or some other game. (If you are not doing so, you should do it!). But, what are the benefits of these activities to you? Obviously, not everyone of you is necessarily planning to become a player or a painter or a singer in your later life. That may, or may not happen. The real intention is to enrich your personality, so that you can appreciate art, take pleasure in music, and enjoy games in your later life. That is the idea.

So, when you learn the technique of quick switch over, what you achieve immediately in your student life is of secondary importance. The formation of a good habit, which is characteristic of all successful people, is important. The intention is to lay the foundation of success and happiness in your later life.

So, here are three starting steps in time management.

1) Analyze your daily routine to understand your existing pattern of spending time.
2) Decide that you reduce 10% of time spent on every activity.
3) The simplest and most effective way of doing this is to develop the habit of quick switch over from one activity to another.

6

Planning Your Day.

The key to successful time management is your ability to plan your day; and your ability to execute that planning.

In fact, this is the key to success in everything that you wish to do in your life.

This requires adopting of some simple techniques. The technique for planning is easy; and we will tell you steps for that.

But what is not easy, and is important is your ability to execute those plans. But we will certainly consider that difficult part also, and tell you some tricks to make it less difficult.

First the easy part: planning for the day. Here again, the most important tool is the same, your diary!

You have already entered your daily routine in the diary for a week. You have analyzed the pattern of how you spend your time, and have decided to reduce the time for every activity by just 10%. Well! Very good!

If we ask, 'what do you want to become in your life later?', or, 'What do you want to achieve in your life?', we are sure most of you will give quick answers. This question is asked very often to most of the children, and they know the answer. (Or, they think they know the answer!) Sometimes the parents or other elders in the family decide for the growing child what he (or she) wishes to become: mostly, a doctor or an engineer! So most of you will quickly say, you want to be a doctor, or an engineer, or an architect, or a chartered accountant or some such thing. Some may, hopefully, also say that they want to become painters or dancers or writers or actors or players!

However, the fact is that most boys and girls at their young age do not really know what they would become, or should become, in their later lives. This was true for the earlier generations; and it is more so for today's generation. This is because; the world is changing very fast and the rate of change is increasing rapidly. Your generation is in a whirl-wind age! New fields and new opportunities are emerging every day. And what was 'new' yesterday is obsolete today, and what is 'new' today will be out-dated tomorrow. Even for a 'futurologist' (the expert who analyzes today's trends; and predicts tomorrow's world) it is difficult to imagine the nature of our society after a few decades from now. So, what you want to become later on in your life, in a sense, becomes a question without much meaning. It can have only a general answer. And the obvious universal answer, true for every one of you is that you want to become a successful person! You want to achieve health, wealth and happiness!

The question today is NOT 'what you want to do in your later life, when you grow up?' The pertinent question in this changing world is, 'what you want to do in the coming 12 months', 'what you want to do this week', 'what you want to do today.' And very few students can give answers to these questions, and the answers are not likely to change from one day to another.

Most people have a dream about their future, and many have a long term plan to persue their dream. But all successful people have an immediate aim, and also a short term plan to pursue that aim. They know what they want to do *today*. All successful students also have stumbled upon this secret, mostly by accident. They know, however, that the important thing is to plan what is to be done today. '*Today*' is the key word for success.

This secret of success is expressed beautifully in a prayer.

Lead kindly light, lead thou my feet.
For I do not want to see the distant scene;
one step enough for me. One step enough for me.

The essence of the key to time management lies in these words: 'One step enough for me!' Do not dwell too much on what you will be doing when you grow up. Life has become so complex, and the world is changing so fast, that what you decide today may become meaningless tomorrow. All that you can decide for the long term future is that you will face challenges and seize opportunities as they come. Detailed long term planning is out.

But that does not mean that short term planning is also out! That does not mean you will not plan for today, or for the week! No, not at all! On the other contrary, short term planning is extremely important. You should be very clear in your mind, as to what you want to do and achieve in the current year, in the current week, and what concretely you want to do today.

That may appear to be simple; but it is not. Most of us are clear (or apparently clear) as to what we want to do, and achieve later on in life, a few years down the line. Most young students know what they will become, when they grow up. Most grown up youths are clear in their minds, as to what they will do when they are settled. Most settled young people are clear, as to what they will do when they become middle aged, and their family responsibilities reduce. Most middle aged people dream of what they will do when they retire. And when people retire, then what? For most of them, life is a list of missed chances and lost opportunities.

So in short, the most important day in your life is TODAY.

Time management means to manage this day, today, in your life. This sentence is so important, that we are going to repeat it. You must memorize this sentence. Repeat it to yourself in your mind over and over again, so that it gets internalized. Perhaps you could paste it on the wall in your home, so that you see it frequently every day.

"TIME MANGEMENT MEANS MANAGING THIS DAY, TODAY, IN MY LIFE."

But, how to manage today? What is the technique?

The technique is simple. In fact it is unbelievably simple. It does not require hard work, or high intelligence. It does not require training or time. All that it requires is commitment and consistency. And, yes! It is very effective and delivers results!

But before we tell you the technique, here is a story that you should read. The story is about the chairman of a big steel company in the US in the first decade of the 20th century. The name of the company is Bthlehem Steel; and Mr.Schewab was the then Chairman of the company. Schewab had a constant uncomfortable feeling of being stressed under work pressure; and a feeling that his time was being consumed on matters of lesser importance, at the cost of more important matters. He asked his consultant Ivy Lee, one of the pioneers in the field of management consultancy. Lee, as the story goes, instantly handed him a blank sheet of paper, and told him to write down the list of jobs he had to attend that day, put their priorities and allot time for every job.

Schewab did that and the uncomfortable feeling was gone. He continued with the practice and the results were astonishing. He recommended the technique to other top executives of the company, and soon he found that work of the company was faster and more organized. He asked Lee, what he expected from the company in return for his suggestion. Lee told him to pay whatever he felt the idea was worth. Lee got a check of $25,000/-. That amount in the first decade of 20th century, more than 100 years back, is worth many million dollars today!

This million dollar idea was nothing but the introduction of the technique of time management in the corporate world. It has since become a part of the corporate culture. All big companies practice this technique, and the more successful ones among them do so more effectively. Also, the technique is being systematically taught to the students of management courses. It has almost become a necessary tool for big wheels in the corporate world, business executives, sales persons, and others. Several other lucky individuals in other fields, who stumbled upon this technique by accident and stuck to it, are benefitted from it. And now it is your turn- dear students- to benefit from it.

So, the tool you need to implement the technique of time management is again the same. That small, inexpensive thing: a diary! And, of course, a pen! Now what you have to do is that you write down the list of things you want to do tomorrow in that diary before you go to bed tonight. Let us call it a 'to-do' list. Simply make a 'to-do' list, i.e. the list of all the activities that you will be doing tomorrow. Put them sequentially, and put the time allotted for each activity. How complete your 'to-do' list is and how realistic you are in assigning time slots for each activity will decide how successful you are in learning the technique of time management. In short, your success lies in your skill in making the 'to-do' list.

Actually, not only time management, but the basic skill of management in any other area also is the skill in making lists! In any case, that is the starting point and that is very crucial.

Suppose a marriage ceremony is being planned in your family. Do you know what your elders start with? Observe carefully. They start with making lists. There is a list of people to whom invitations are to be sent, then a list of what purchases are to be made, a list of menu items to be finalized, a list of what things are to be ordered for decoration, a list of what special items are to be procured for the marriage rituals, a list of gifts to be given to close and elderly relatives, and a list of this, and a list of that! The more detailed are the lists, the more planned is the function. Also note that all the lists are actually *written down* on a paper, or preferably in a notebook.

When a big research project is being planned, (say the project of putting a man on the moon, or that of developing and marketing new software; etc.) or when a big factory is being constructed, do you know the first step all these projects start with? It is by preparing a 'bar chart'. A bar chart is nothing but a detailed list of the sequence of steps to be taken to meet the target (in other words, a detailed and very long 'to-do' list); and a time slot for completing each item in the list. The time slot is put in the form of horizontal 'bar' in front of every activity denoting the number of days in which that activity is to be completed (Hence the name 'bar chart'). Thus a bar chart is a modified version of the 'to-do' list for a complex project.

So from carrying out a mission of putting a man on the moon to constructing a factory and running it smoothly, to organizing a function in a family, everywhere making a 'to-do' list is the crucial starting step.

Why is the making of lists for different projects so important?

This is because, the lists are liberating. When you are writing down the list of things to be done to complete a job, you must sit quietly at a place and think with concentration about all aspects of that job. Remember, you have to note down every little thing, big or small, that comes to your mind regarding completion of the job. You also think of the sequence in which those activities related with the job are to be done, and the time required for each activity. This is like mapping the path in advance with all the details, before starting an expedition.

If this crucial part is not done with concentration in the beginning before you start with the job, then you may suddenly remember midcourse that something has not been done in time, and it then has to be done immediately. It then becomes an urgency. Or you may realize that something essential has not been done in time; and it is then too late. It then becomes an emergency. The recurrence of the states of urgency and emergency will create confusion and stress.

A systematically prepared advance 'to-do' list avoids this confusion and stress. You are less likely to encounter unpleasant surprises in completing the project. You are free from any kind of tension in your mind. That is why the lists are liberating.

When confusion and tension enter your mind, the first casualty is your confidence. You start losing your confidence. You continuously start doubting, whether things are going in the right direction and with the proper speed. You get stressed. A constant nagging thought haunts your mind that you are missing out something important and that it is going to land you in trouble.

If you have a well thought out and a detailed 'to-do' list containing all the steps to be taken at every stage of the job, then, in the first place, there is no reason why this stress and these nagging thoughts should trouble you. But, if they do start troubling you, then your 'to-do' list is a miraculous medicine for that! Simply look at the list, and confirm that things are going as planned; or exactly pinpoint which activity is lagging behind, and take steps to rectify the situation. No tension, no confusion, no loss of confidence!

Thus lists are a confidence booster. People who prepare exhaustive 'to-do' lists are always calm and quiet and tension free while carrying out any job, big or small. No wonder, they often succeed in their mission. What is important is that they exude confidence. Not only do they succeed, they *know from the beginning* that they are going to succeed! As a result, leadership of any project very often lands in their hands. They are appreciated by their colleagues and others especially because of the aura of self-assurance they carry with them.

Sometimes the very simplicity of an idea is its handicap. The novelty of an idea may be lost because of its simplicity. There is an anecdote in this connection. In a party, a man asked a riddle to others present. 'Take this boiled egg', he said, 'and keep it on this table so that one of its tapering ends is pointing upward.' All the others tried it in different ways, but failed. The egg would always lie flat on the table with its both tapering ends pointing in the horizontal direction. Ultimately, they turned the man to do it. What did the man do? He quietly picked up a knife, and cut the boiled egg in the middle into two halves. Then he put the two halves on the table with their flat sides on the table and tapering sides pointing upwards! 'Here it is!', said the man. 'The tapering sides are pointing up'!

'Oh! That is simple', remarked others.

'Yes!' replied the man, 'that is simple; but not obvious. Effective ideas are often simple, but they are not obvious'.

Frequently, simple solutions are not appreciated, because they are dismissed as being too simple. But, in reality simple solutions are usually the best solutions. 'To keep yourself fit, you must exercise regularly' tell the doctors. And which exercise should we choose? Walking! What a simple answer! But that is the best answer according to doctors. The reason why we explained at length how the idea of making 'to-do' lists is effective and powerful, is because its simplicity may turn you off. The idea is not trivial, though it may appear to be so to an inexperienced mind. It is most certainly a very effective idea and dividends are quick and plenty.

Remember, Ivy Lee got a check of $ 25000, more than hundred years ago for suggesting this idea? Now, the people in the corporate world are very calculating and careful while making payments to anybody and spending their money. The chairman of a steel company would surely not squander millions of dollars (in today's terms) for a trivial idea. So, please don't be misled by the simplicity of the idea.

Some of you may say, 'O. K.! It is a good idea. Not a trivial one. But, for whom is it intended?' You might further think that, 'it is, no doubt, useful for the captains of the industry, or for the leaders of big research projects and for high level executives. They have to prepare 'to-do' lists, and draw bar charts, because they have big and challenging jobs to do. They are busy professionals. They have to keep track of many things and meet many people every day. But, I am just a student. I hardly have such a busy schedule. Why do I need to prepare lists of my daily routine activities? Why should I write them down? I am quite capable of remembering them.'

You are almost right, but not quite! It is correct that industry captains, top level executives, high government officials, powerful politicians, great artists and scientists, and all such big and successful people from all walks of life have more challenging jobs to do. They have very busy schedules of visits, meetings, and so on. Most of them do have a practice of preparing their daily 'to do' lists. It is also true that very few ordinary people follow this practice. But it is incorrect to conclude that the habit of preparing daily 'to do' lists was acquired by the big and successful people, *after* they became big and successful. They became big and successful, *because* they had earlier developed the habit of preparing daily 'to-do' lists. Do not confuse between the cause and the effect. The 'habit' is the cause and the 'success' is the effect. Also, those few 'ordinary' people today who have developed the habit of making and following daily 'to-do' lists, will surely rise to higher and higher levels of success, and it is only a matter of time before they become 'big' and successful.

You do not wait to become big and successful to acquire the working habits of successful people. You acquire those habits, so that the success comes to your door, searching your address. Sachin Tendulkar did not wait to learn his batting technique, and practice his powerful shots, until he became a distinguished batsman. He did not wait to develop his life style which gave him sustained stamina and robust mental strength until he became the topmost batsman of the world. He learnt his technique, practiced his shots and developed his life style before, and as a result he became 'Sachin Tendulkar, The Great'. So beware of this common pitfall—'confusing between the cause and the effect'.

If you start preparing your daily 'to do' lists right from this age, you will start early on the path of achieving success in whichever field you choose to pursue later in your life. Also, you will soon discover that your leadership qualities will become prominent from your student days and will take you to greater heights later in your life. In short the project we are talking about is to make you a confident, successful person with leadership qualities.

And, now tell me, what bigger project could be there than this one? Putting a man on the moon is also secondary to the project of carving a confident and competent person from a student on the earth. Especially, if that student is YOU! Remember, no other project is more important than this. This is *the* project, in which you have to succeed. And all efforts must be undertaken; all techniques must be adopted to see that success is achieved. Failure here is simply not allowed. There could be failure in an examination; there could be failure in getting admission to a course of your choice. These failures are temporary difficulties and you can tide over them. But there cannot be a failure in the project of developing you into a confident and competent person.

So, here is the first and the most important step on time management: purchase a small diary and prepare every day 'to-do' lists.

We want to reemphasize the point made before. Do not be misled by simplicity of the suggestion. Resolve to implement it. Basically, it is not difficult. You have already carried out the exercise of 'know thyself' for the last about two weeks, in which you have recorded the activities that you carry out every day (and the time required for each activity). Admittedly, most of the activities will be repetitive. But still record them in your 'to do' list. Then there will be some small things, which you are sure that you will remember. But, do record them. Make the list as exhaustive as possible.

Here is an example of a 'to-do' list of one of the students.

Vikas is a student of std. VIII, and is a fairly good student. He is not the topper in his class, but he is among the top ten. He also has interests in many other activities in the school. How would one of his days in the school get reflected in the 'to-do' list? We give below an example of his 'to-do' list, with our comments in the brackets.

6.00am: To get up from the bed.

6 to 6.35: Morning chores. (Earlier time 40 mins. By 10% formula, reduced to 35 mins.)

6.35 to 6.40: Morning Prayer or 'session of positive thinking' (We will tell you about this in a later chapter, but this is a very powerful tool. Note that he took out time for this from our 10% formula.)

6.40 to 6.45: Get ready for school.

6.45 to7: Reach the school.

7 to 12.30: School.

——Return the notebook of Science to Archana.

——check for thermometers in the lab for science project.

——ask difficulties to the history teacher.

——congratulate Suresh for his good innings in the cricket match yesterday.

——Find out from the office, details about the scholarship forms.

(Note that the regular class time table is not included in this list. The *additional* things that Vikas wants to do on a particular day are included. Also, no entry in itself is of any special nature. All are simple and routine. Surely, you are doing these or other similar things routinely on any day in your school or college. What is different is that Vikas spent a few minutes on the *previous* night to think of his day *tomorrow*, and jotted down the activities. He *planned* his tomorrow. That is the key. On any one day, the advantages of this technique are not noticeable; but there would be a distinct cumulative effect over a few weeks, and this would increase with time. Everyone including Vikas, will soon realize that he is doing everything that needs to be done; and is doing it in time.)

Vikas's school gets over at 12.30 pm. He then has a planned schedule of activities for the rest of the day, which is as given below.

Vikas comes home, takes his lunch and then relaxes until 2.00pm. He refers to his 'to do' list again after lunch, to see if there is something that can be done, while he is relaxing. He notices two things from the list. He has to call his aunt, Neema Mausi, because he has not talked to her for a long time; and he wants to download a new song on his mobile. Vikas decides to make a call to Neema Mausi now. (The other thing will also be done today; but at a later time). He indulges in some small talk to her; and asks her about her health, and about the activities of her small children, his cousins. There is nothing particularly important in that conversation, but Neema Mausi is pleased. She calls Vikas as her most lovable nephew, and praises him because he always finds time to call her. Vikas is also pleased, and his time of relaxation is spent fruitfully, and in an enriching manner. And this is basically because of the list he had made the previous night.

Precisely at 2.00pm Vikas goes to his study table. In his broad time table, he has devoted the time of 2.00pm to 5.00pm for studies. He has also jotted down points about study in his 'to do' list. Vikas looks at the broad time table. The time from 2.00pm to 3.00pm is for revising what was taught in the school that day. This actually takes less time, because whatever was taught recently is fresh in mind, and does not take much time to revise. Vikas quickly goes through the lessons in the text book, notes in his note book and, wherever necessary modifies the notes taken down in the class. He also sees the mathematical formulae discussed in the class, and the sums solved in the class.

From experience, Vikas knows that this revision takes less time, if done on the same day. If it is carried out the next day, it takes double the time; and if the time gap is more than one day, it is really very difficult to remember and revise whatever that was taught in the class. (This is a very important point. Always revise at home, whatever was taught in the class that very day, or the next day. Do not delay it further. It will greatly reduce the time of revision, and will improve your preparation of that topic. It is an effective way for good time management, and achieving better results with less time spent.) He also completes his home-work given by teachers on that day. (This is another good habit for saving time, and avoiding tension. Do your home work, preferably, on the day it is given; or may be, the next day, if something else is to be completed urgently on that day. But never prolong it beyond that. It takes more time to complete the same work, if prolonged. That is bad time management.)

Fifteen minutes after three, his revision and home work get completed. (Vikas knows from experience that this part of revising and completing of home work does take a little extra time on some days; or gets completed in shorter time on some other days. But, while preparing the time table for studies, he and his mother thoughtfully decided that the first hour of study every day must be allotted for revision and home work.

Vikas then takes some time for refreshing himself before starting a new subject. He takes a short break before he goes back to study. ('*Short*' is the key word in that sentence.) Vikas just takes a round of all the rooms in his small house, sings one of his favorite film songs, splashes cold water on his face, drinks a glass of water and so on and so forth. Vikas has learnt from experience that such small things which bring in a momentary break in activity really refresh him. (You can also try it. But a word of caution! The break in activity should be only *momentary*. Avoid picking up a news paper at that time, and never switch on a T.V., or make a phone call. These activities can never remain momentary. They will eat away a lot of your time allotted for studies.)

Vikas then studies a lesson from science up to 4pm as is listed in his time table. He uses the method of 'speak out' while doing this. (We will tell you more about this method in a later chapter. It is an effective way of studying faster and better.) He then again takes a break of 5 minutes, and looks at the time table for that day. Well, the day is Monday; and he finds that on Mondays, 4 to 5 pm is the time slot for studying English. He has to complete that new poem from the text book of English as per the plan; and has to learn it by heart. But then he remembers that the mathematics teacher had taught a new lesson that day, which was not easy. The teacher had said that the sums in that lesson were very challenging; and that students should practice as many sums as possible. Vikas strongly feels that he should open the mathematics text book, rather than the English textbook that day. 'English can be studied later', he thinks to himself. He knows that, occasionally, if the situation so demands, changes can be done in the time table. 'And any way, I am not wasting time. I am going to use it for studies as planned. Just that it is mathematics instead of English that was planned earlier', Vikas speaks to himself.

He is about to open his Mathematics text book, and settle to study, when the phone rings. His mother is calling from her office. 'Yes, dear', she asks, 'are you comfortable? Are you spending time in your studies, as per the time-table?'

'Yes, Mom', replies Vikas, 'the thing is that I am making a small change in the schedule. Instead of English, I am using the time to study mathematics. You know Mom, the time table is only a guide line, and changes can be done, if we so desire. And there is no harm, when the time allotted for study is spent on study, and not on anything else. Isn't it Mom?'

'Listen, my child', the mother replies from the other end. 'I have an important meeting to attend now and I don't have much time to talk now. We will talk later in the evening when I come home. But do one thing now. Do your studies exactly as per the time table. No changes today. Ok? If it is English in the time table, then it is English today! Clear? And we will talk in the evening'. The mother hangs up the phone.

Vikas is not happy with this conversation. Actually, he is angry with his mother. But he decides to comply by what she asked him to do. He opens his English text book and is engrossed with it up to 5 pm. Then he freshens up, eats some tasty and sumptuous snacks, down loads that latest song in his mobile and then goes to Hiren's place. His other friends also arrive. Vikas tells them about the new song in his mobile. They start discussing the science project. 'Oh!', one of the boys suddenly remembers and remarks, 'we have to find out about the thermometers in the school. We discussed it last time, and then forgot about it.' 'No', says Vikas, 'I went to the lab today and found out. Thermometers of the range we want are available in our school.' 'That's good', says Hiren, 'Vikas you are really great. You have done an important thing in time.' Everyone else agrees. They spend time discussing and deciding about the science project.

After dinner that night, his mother talks to Vikas. 'Listen Vikas,' she says, 'You studied mathematics instead of English two weeks ago. That time there was one reason. Today you wanted to do that for some other reason. The fact is that you like mathematics more than languages. There is nothing wrong in that. Later on you can choose to study mathematics at higher level. But today, when you are in school, you must study all other subjects with equal interest. And remember one thing. Though, we can change the timetable, if necessary, we must do it very rarely. We have prepared it with some thinking behind it; and it has some meaning, only if we follow it rigorously. Sometimes following the timetable may appear to create temporary problems and hardships and we may be tempted to change it. And this may happen frequently. But, as far as possible, we must avoid that. Making a time table and preparing 'to do' lists are good habits. But their fruits are enjoyed only by those who respect the timetables and honor the lists.'

As per his schedule, Vikas spends time in watching his favorite TV program, spends some time in reading the story book he has brought from library and then sits at his study table again with his diary. He tick marks the items from the 'to-do' list which were completed. Most of the things were done. He then spends time and prepares his 'to-do' list of the next day. When he goes to bed, he feels very happy and contented, because he has done most of the things which were planned for that day, and he knows what he wants to do the next day.

What Vikas likes the best about his 'to-do' lists is to make tick marks on completed items at the end of the day. Almost always most of the items are done (because most of them are individually simple and routine items); but that gives him a great satisfaction of having spent the day successfully! And this feeling boosts his confidence tremendously.

Also, Vikas is lucky because he has a mother who has understood the essence of time management. And he is wise because he listens to his mother. What Vikas's mother was telling him can be said to be the most crucial factor in time management. Making of the 'to do' list is important. Preparing a time table for studies is important. But, what is most important is to follow that time table, and to respect that list. Therefore, for succeeding in time management, do a simple thing. Keep on repeating the following statements to yourself as many times as possible, in a day.

'I have written a plan for today, and I shall succeed in following that plan.'

'I will complete my 'to do' list today. That is very easy; and also very important for me.'

Repeat these statements to yourself again and again. Repeat them at least ten times every day in the morning. Repeat them in your mind after every one hour. Repeat them regularly for days and months. They should become a part of your personality trait, your nature. And once that happens, your success in acquiring skills of time management is guaranteed.

You see, sometimes there are genuine difficulties in following the plan of a day. There are genuine problems in completing the 'to do' list of the day. Sometimes some items in the 'to do' list of today have to be postponed to some other day, due to circumstances beyond your control. So, there is nothing wrong, if every single item on the 'to do' list of the day is not completed on that day. A few items may remain. But we should be able to cover majority of items.

Also, don't be too ambitious in preparing the 'to do' list. There are limits on what you can do in a day, and the list should accordingly be prepared. The list should not be heavily loaded, nor should it be too short. Also, today is not the last day in your life! So, it is not necessary that everything be done today. At the same time, there is always a temptation to postpone to tomorrow things which can be done today. This is called procrastination. 'Procrastination' is your worst enemy. And, particularly it is the greatest hazard to the project of time management.

One of the basic purposes of teaching you time management in your student days is to keep you away from the monster of procrastination from an early age. The victims affected by this monster have to be freed from its clutches first. So, on the one hand, things which are to be done today, or which can be done today should not be postponed to tomorrow. On the other hand, everything should not be planned to be done in one day. It may unnecessarily lead to confusion and mental stress. The stress may also adversely affect the quality of work. Care must be taken to see that the daily 'to do' list is not too heavy, nor too light.

How to ensure that? Well! There is no standard formula for this. Only experience will tell you the appropriate length of the list. You simply start with making the 'to do' list. Make it as detailed, as complete as possible. Include apparently simple items also. And try to complete the list with utmost sincerity. If a few things remain to be done, it is ok! You can include them in the list prepared for tomorrow.

On some occasions, there are problems and difficulties. Judge whether they can be solved and whether, in spite of difficulties, you can follow the plan of the day. Try hard to complete the 'to do' list of the day. When faced with adversities, treat them as a challenge. Do not accept the defeat easily. Treat it as a game in your mobile, where the player has to reach the goal (completing the 'to do' list) against all odds. Finally, in spite of the difficulties, if you can complete the list, you will feel happy and elated, as you feel when you win a game. If you do not succeed on a particular day, you will decide that on the next day you are going to win the game!

So, you can consider Time Management as a game you are playing with the mighty flow of Time. It tests your will power to achieve your goal. And what is the goal? It simply is to complete your 'to-do' list of that day. If you do not win on one day, you will definitely win the next day! No doubt about that.

So, what are you waiting for? Start the game from today. Prepare your 'to do' list. And, yes, start repeating the mantra of Time Management.

So, what are the basic things for time management?

Have a diary.

Write down your 'to do' list in it every day.

Prepare time table for your studies at home.

Treat learning the skill of Time Management as a game you are playing with the mighty flow of Time.

Keep repeating the mantra of time management in your mind as often as possible.

The mantra of Time Management is again given below.

'I have written a plan for today, and I shall succeed in following that plan.'

'I will complete my 'to do' list today. That is very easy; and also very important for me.'

7

Small Steps and the Big Picture.

What is the smallest number? Well! The answer to that is easy. It is 'zero'.

What is the biggest number?

Now, that is a difficult one! This question has no answer. You think of any big number. It may be the total number of stars in the sky, or the total number of water molecules in the oceans, or whatever! Give me any number, however big, and I can give a number bigger than that. There is nothing like the biggest number in mathematics. (There is a term called 'infinity' in mathematics, but it is not a number. It is a device to incorporate the fact in theories of mathematics, that there is always a number, bigger than any given number.)

Further, do you know something? Our ability to write bigger and bigger numbers is due to the smallest number zero. Without the discovery of 'zero' in the number system (which by the way, is a contribution of India to the world), big and bigger and still bigger numbers could not have been so easily written and counted, as we do now.

Also, there is one more interesting thing.

One zero is zero, the lowest number.

Two zeros are also zero, the lowest number.

But just add 'one' before the two zeroes, and it becomes 'hundred'!

It is a big number.

It is the 'century' in cricket, desired by every batsman.

It is the percentage of marks, desired by every student in every examination.

It is the age up to which we desire our near and dear ones should live.

So, the two zeros independently have no value; but they become big and important, when they are a part of 'hundred'.

You might be wondering, what is this going on here? Why have we suddenly turned to the teaching of mathematics, while the topic of discussion is 'time management'? But, what we want to point out is something beyond mathematics, something more general and profound. Here are two general principles of life, two basic laws of nature.

One: you can handle 'big', if you can handle 'small'.

Two: The 'small' becomes significant, only when it is a part of a big picture.

These same two principles are important in time management too.

So, the first thing to realize is that 'small is crucial'. There is a famous maxim in English, 'Small is beautiful'. The maxim in time management is, 'Small is crucial'. What it means is that even small daily activities have crucial importance. As a matter of fact, most of your daily activities, if considered in bits, are apparently small and insignificant. You may tend to neglect such small actions while preparing your daily 'to do' lists. You may think that instead of such routine and small items, your 'to do' lists should contain some impressive and special items. But this feeling is wrong. Actually, the list should mostly, or even entirely, contain normal, routine, small items. That, in fact, is a good list! That is welcome. When you start preparing long and exhaustive 'to do' lists, you have achieved a major success in time management. Because, that would mean you have developed an ability to pay attention to details. It would mean, you have learnt the importance of handling and planning small things. This is *the* ability of all successful people that underlies their success. Planning all the details carefully and working out those plans faithfully is the recipe of success. Neglecting the planning of details is often the cause of failure. There are many people who work hard and possess a strong desire to succeed; but they do not succeed. A careful analysis of their failure shows that in nine cases out of ten, the reason for it was simply their neglect of details, neglect of seemingly small things.

There is a story in this connection, as to how a war was lost.

At the peak of a crucial battle, a nail from the horse shoe of a horse came out on the battle field. The horse could not move easily on the field.

For want of a nail, the horse was lost.

For want of a horse a warrior was lost.

For want of a warrior the battle was lost.

Due to loss in the battle, the morale of the army was lost.

For want of morale, the war was lost.

Thus, in the final analysis, for want of a nail, the war was lost!

This happens in every walk of life. The battle need not be on a battle field. It may be a battle to complete some project in any field. A small mistake, a small deficiency can cause a big loss, and the battle can be lost.

Therefore, paying attention to details is important. And the best way to do that is to include the details, however trivial they may look, in your 'to do' lists. You see, you can cover a large distance, if you cover the next one meter in proper direction; and that is true for every meter. You can climb to the top of a hill, but for that you have to take the next step upwards. For scoring a century, the most important thing for a batsman is to face the next ball with confidence.

So, take care of small things. Take care of details. In time management, this means take care of TODAY. The key word in management technique is TODAY. You see, the past is over and gone forever. No one, not even God the Almighty can change the past. The future is a mystery. It is surrounded by the mist of unknown factors, and we can only dream about it. But TODAY is here. It is in our hand. We are experiencing it. We can shape it. It is the only time, we can work in. 'Today' is the gift given by the God to every one of us. That is why, it is called 'present'. So, the basic two rules of time management are: plan today, and plan even seemingly trivial details. The technique for that is to prepare exhaustive 'to do' lists every day; and to honor them.

But that is not all. There is something more. We want to make an important addition to the technique of making 'to do' lists; and that is the need of having a 'big picture' before your eyes. Small things that we incorporate in our daily 'to do' lists acquire significance only if they are part of a big picture. Remember, the lowest number 'zero' becomes significant only when it is associated with a big number? Every run scored by a batsman is important; but it becomes really significant when the final score is a century. The same is true in life. Your success in acquiring skill of time management is meaningful only when it is aimed at some 'big picture'. The tools of time management that we have discussed, and are going to discuss later on, are just that: they are tools. They are the techniques. But the real meaning to time management is acquired, when a big picture is in place.

And what is meant by the 'Big Picture'? It simply is a larger goal that you set for yourself. It is the dream for your life.

Once you decide the larger goal, you can plan the path forward. Remember the big picture is your own, your personal goal. No one else can see your dream for you! No one else can paint the big picture for you! You alone must do it. But, yes! Some general possibilities can be discussed.

Suppose your dream is to become a scientist. Then that is your 'big picture', your larger goal. Now, the next thing is to decide your path forward. That is, to convert the larger goal into smaller steps, leading you to the final destination. This is not easy. It requires knowledge about the field of your interest. It needs judgment about what is possible, and what is not possible. It needs information about opportunities available to students. You, obviously, cannot have this knowledge, information and judgment right at the start. So, you must seek help from others. You must discuss your aim with some experienced elders and some experts in the field. The best persons to discuss this are your teachers. A teacher is always ready to help her students. She may encourage you to take part in science project exhibitions held every year. She may tell you about the 'Homi Bhabha examinations'; or the 'National Talent Search' Examination held for students every year. Also, your parents, or someone known to them, may have information about the field of science, whom you can consult. Also, now-a-days, the internet is a big source of information. Some elders in the family can do that job for you.

Or, suppose you want to become a writer in your later life. Then you must read great authors and good books. Again, you can consult your language teacher to decide which authors and which books to read; and about how to practice writing during your school days. You can get opinion about whatever you write from someone in the family who is a good reader, or a writer.

If your school has a 'wall paper', you can start contributing to that. If there is no 'wall paper' in the school, you can take a lead and start one. It will give you a good practice of writing regularly; and also a good exposure to your writing.

Suppose your aim is to become an army officer. Then, obviously, physical fitness among other things is a must for you. You must work for a healthy body and a strong mind and this needs much self-control. (This is, of course, needed for success in every profession). To become an army officer, you must cultivate a bold attitude to face adversities and a strong will power to achieve any given target. You may again have to take advice from your physical training instructor in the school and others who know about the army. You may have to start a proper regime of exercise and fitness training. You will have to join the unit of Scout or N.C.C.

If your big picture is to become a singer, or a dancer; you must join music or dance classes.

But, if your big picture is to become an actor, or an actress, there is a word of caution for you! You may then spend a lot of time watching TV programs and movies; seriously believing that by doing so, you are working towards achieving your goal! Nothing could be more incorrect. Actually, becoming an actor or an actress is a tough goal; and requires much hard work. It requires a good physique, an impressive personality and a good command over dialogue delivery. This requires systematic effort and proper guidance. Watching movies and copying actions or stiles of heroes is not the way. No successful actor has ever copied someone else. If your aim is to join acting profession, then take part in skits presented in your school or college. Join workshops to learn acting. Be a part of the group, when rehearsals for skits are going on.

We explained this point at some length, because in today's world, many of you may have been blinded by the glamour of film world, and may be dreaming of getting into it. Remember, it is not easy. The path is full of cut-throat competition, and requires very hard work. And most importantly, never deceive yourself by imagining that spending time in seeing movies and watching TV serials is the path towards that goal.

To continue our main discussion, the 'Big Picture' for many of you may be to become a doctor, or an engineer, or a Chartered Accountant, or an architect or some such professional. Perhaps most of you have such an aim. That is quite natural. The society needs writers and scientists and artists, but it also needs competent professionals; and that too in far greater numbers. So, if your aim is to become a professional, then what are the steps?

Well, they are simple; in the sense, they are well defined. If you want to become a professional then you must study hard, understand the examination technique and strive to get good marks in the examination! But if you want to become a *good* professional, then something more is required. You must then have the qualities of leadership. You must be able to express your views clearly. You should have good communication skills, and should be able to convince others of your views.

So, the 'Big Picture' has many answers, many possibilities. Every individual has a right to have his or her own dream, different from others. Think of your own dream today. You are still very young and have little experience of life. Life is so complex, that your dream may change with time. The actual profession or activity, which you will take up later in your life, may not be the same as the one in your big picture. That does happen sometimes; and is not to be treated as a failure. As a famous song goes,

'*Ke cera cera,*
whatever will be, will be!'

But right now you must have a big picture before your eyes, and you must sincerely pursue it. That creates a tremendous driving force during your student days. It motivates you. And the efforts you take to achieve that goal are not wasted. They bring positive energy. They bring desirable changes in your personality. They enrich your life. Actually, the efforts towards reaching the goal are more valuable than reaching the goal itself.

The main thing is, after you decide on your 'big picture'; paint it! That is, work on it. Collect relevant details by discussing with your teachers, elders in your family and experts. Internet is a great source of up-to-date information. You can access the information yourself, or seek the help of some elders in the family for that purpose. You should mainly concentrate on those details, which would be useful in deciding your course of actions for the next one or two years. *'Course of actions'* is the key phrase here. Because collecting the information is not the real project. In the days of internet, it can happen that you get so much information on any topic in just a few seconds that it will take years, if you decide to read every word of it! What is important is to decide an informed course of action to reach the goal. Put these actions in small steps, and in details. Use the last two pages of your diary for this purpose.

So, your diary of 'to do' lists will also contain a small description of your 'big picture' and a list of the steps you intend to take over a period of, say, next six months to one year to achieve your goal. This list should be upgraded or modified occasionally, as required. This is not an 'every day' list. You can glance through it, may be once in fifteen days, or one month. The steps included in this 'big picture' list may not directly appear in your daily 'to do' lists. But they will be reflected in it indirectly.

For example, Vikas is more interested in science, and his big picture is to become a scientist, or an engineer. That is why he has entries in his 'to do' list, as we have seen earlier, about science project, and checking of thermometers in the school lab. Archana, on the other hand has an ambition to become a writer. There would be entries, therefore, in her daily 'to do' lists, which read like, 'to get the book of Mahabharata by C. Rajgopalachari', or 'to discuss with the Head Mistress regarding notice board allocation for wall paper'. Juli's big picture is to become a sports person. Her entries in 'to do' lists will correspond to the sports practice timings and such other matters related to sports.

The point is, these details will appear in your daily 'to do' lists, which independently are small and insignificant. But they become significant, when they are part of the big picture that you have before your eyes. Remember, the 'zeroes' in mathematics are independently insignificant, but they have a large value when they are part of a bigger number.

So, the next rule for time management is: 'have a big picture before your eyes, collect some relevant information and decide an action plan for it for the next one or two years, and *write down* this big picture and the plan of action on the last two pages of your diary.'

8

How to Study.

The most important thing in the life of a student is his 'academic studies'. Whatever may be his other achievements, the success of a student is always measured by his success in academic studies and examinations. The 'failure' of a student means his inability to succeed in an examination. So, whatever else you may do successfully, you cannot afford to neglect your studies. You have to be good at it. Study is the *dharma* of a student. It is the main duty of a student. Your project of learning 'time management' has real value, only if it makes you more efficient in your academic studies, more successful in your examinations, and gives you time to pursue other fields of your interest, without affecting your studies.

So, we will tell you some simple techniques, which will save your time of study and make the process more efficient. But first, let us talk about a magic formula. Yes, there is a magic formula for success in studies. In fact, it is the formula for success in any walk of life. It is a universal formula, which any one can apply and become successful. It is an ancient magic formula, which has been told in ancient books of wisdom. But it needs to be repeated again and again, especially to every new generation.

So, here we tell you the magic formula for success. Pay attention carefully!

The magic formula is: 'Hard Work'!

Oh! We can see the disappointment on your face! 'This is unfair'! 'This is an anticlimax'! 'Where is the magic, if there is hard work'? That is what you feel, and rightly so.

But wait, wait! We want to add something to this formula. The complete magic formula is, 'Hard Work with Strategy'.

Now, that *is* different. That is not an often repeated formula for success. What is meant by 'strategy'? How does it help in ensuring success? And what is its relation with the time management? Well! We will answer these questions.

But first we talk about the first two words of the formula, 'Hard Work'. So, the formula tells us, that there is no substitute for hard work. Success cannot come without hard work. If someone tells you that success will be awaiting at your door step, if you just carry a 'lucky' stone, or if you carry out a particular ritual; be sure, you are being cheated. No success ever comes by following rituals and carrying lucky stones or any such thing. Success only comes through hard work.

But then why do we add the word 'strategy' to it?

You see, success can come only when there is hard work.., but hard work alone does not guarantee success.

Every success is built on hard work; but every hard work does not result into success.

In the language of mathematics, hard work is a necessary, but not sufficient, condition of success.

The part regarding 'strategy' is to ensure that 'hard work' is converted into success.

What is the best formula for scoring runs in cricket?

Hit the ball hard, what else?

Yes, that is true. But hitting the ball is necessary, not sufficient to score runs.

There is something called 'perfect placement' of the ball.

Only when the placement is perfect, the ball rushes to the boundary; otherwise it goes straight towards a fielder and is stopped. The shot is wasted. Hitting the ball so that the shot yields runs is the 'strategy' part of a successful batsman.

The same is true in every field of life; and for students, particularly it is true for their studies. Hard work must be accompanied by a 'strategy'. With strategy, it is possible to study more effectively with less effort and in less time than without a strategy. Note the words *'less time'*. That is a great boon for time management.

This then should be great news for you, dear students! We print it in bold letters!

'Yes! It is possible to study more effectively in *less time*, and with less effort.'

And there is no magic involved in it. It is simply a question of adopting a proper technique for your studies. Follow the methods described here; and you will see wonderful results. There is a statement in English which highlights the importance of 'strategy'. 'Successful people do not do different things. They only do things differently.'

This sentence is so important, that we are going to repeat it. You should also repeat it to yourself many times. We want you to remember it. What is the statement?

'Successful people do not do different things. They only do the things differently'

In academic studies, there are 'good and successful' students in any class of any school/ college; and there are 'poor and failing' students in the same class of the same school/ college.

Both these types of students study the same subjects, use the same books and have the same teachers. Also, though there could be some difference between the levels of intelligence of two persons, this cannot account for the wide gap in performance of students who excel and those who fail.

The real reason for the difference between performances of the two groups lies in their methods of study. Students who excel in their studies have stumbled upon some secrets of the effective methods of study, others have not. This group has discovered the 'strategy', the other has not. Here now, we will explain this method, this strategy in simple and clear words. We will tell you how to study, so that you understand the subject better, you remember the matter during examinations, and you save time while doing this.

Also, one more point again. Some of the techniques explained here are rather simple. Some of the points will appear (and are) obvious. But let not that simplicity deceive you. These techniques are effective. They work. And the only way to see that they work is to follow them. What is important is to put them all together in totality, as we have done; and to understand them in totality as you will do. So, let us start.

The first point is now familiar to you. We mentioned it earlier. So, we will not spend much time on it. The point is that you must have a time table for your studies. You have already studied your daily routine. Find out the best and maximum time slot for your studies. Divide the total time into 'periods' of fifty minutes. Devote the first one period to revising whatever that was taught in the school that day. Remember, you are not studying that portion in detail. You are only revising. Open your text books and go through the lessons taught in the school that day. Also, look at the notes you might have taken in the school that day. The notes need not be exhaustive. They may contain the main points, key words, important steps, etc. If required, add some small explanations and some remaining key words to the notes. But remember 'notes' do not mean lengthy descriptions, or full answers to questions asked in the examinations. Notes are a tool to remember the topic, as it was discussed in the class, or is discussed in the book. (Later on, there is a chapter on how to take notes.)

So, revise the portion taught in the school that day. If you keep in mind this discussion on 'revising' and 'notes', you will realize that the time of fifty five minutes is sufficient for this revision. If necessary, you may extend this time by 15-20 minutes on a particular day. If you find that you regularly require more time for this revision, then increase the time to about seventy five to ninety minutes (but not beyond that in any case).

Now allot the remaining periods to different subjects. Take difficult subjects in earlier time slots, and easier ones later. This is because you can concentrate better on difficult subjects, when your mind is fresh.

After one subject or one activity, take a small break of about five minutes. The break will enable you to get fresh before you start your next period of study. Do some small activity, which will keep you fresh. A few sips of water, or some juice, if possible; humming of a song to yourself, just sitting quiet and relaxed, and having deep breathing, taking a round within your home are some of the activities we suggest. Making a phone call to your friend, picking up a news paper, switching on TV, lying down on bed are the activities to be avoided at any cost in that break. This is because these activities will extend far beyond five minutes, without you realizing it.

Give some initial period of two weeks and check whether the time table is appropriate, and whether you have given enough time to each subject. Freeze the time table after two weeks with changes, if required. Now start following the time table faithfully. You can make occasional changes in it, but do so only when they are absolutely essential. The best thing is to involve your parents in the project of making the time table. They will judge better whether you are giving proper time to every subject; and whether the changes you wish to do in the time table on any particular day are justified. We have seen what happened on one day in case of Vikas. His mother fortunately called him in time, and gave him proper advice. But it may not happen in every case every time. So, we suggest, the best rule would be that any change in the timetable should be with prior permission of your parents; or some elder in the family, who is competent to do this job.

Make at least two copies of the time table after it is finalized. Keep one copy in your school bag, so that you can refer it in school, if required. Keep the other at your study table. Preferably, paste it on the wall at your place of study. And yes, have a regular place where you study at home. Do not keep changing places of study. This is important as a 'habit forming' technique. The place must be free from distractions. Do not sit facing a window. You will be often tempted to see outside and you may get distracted. Also, for obvious reasons, avoid the room where TV set is located in your house. Remember TV is the biggest source of distraction. It is the greatest hindrance in the project of learning time management.

So, you have prepared a balanced time table for your study, fixed proper time to study every subject, and have decided the regular place where you will study. Then, what next?

Well, the next step is to start studying! What else?

But, then how do you study? Is there any method for studying? That is a million dollar question! You want to know that method for studying, which saves your time, gives you confidence and guarantees success in examinations. When you learn time management as a student, you should naturally expect this. So, is there any such method? That is the real question.

The answer to that question is, 'Yes, there is such a method! There is a method for studying which satisfies all your above requirements'. We are now going to explain that method, which saves time, and ensures success. What is more, this method is not of rote learning, where you may score marks without understanding. This method encourages understanding and comprehension. We have termed this method of studying **'The FITT Method!'**

'FITT' method has four steps:

1) The first step is 'F'.

'F' stands for 'Foreseeing': Get the layout of the lesson and get the general impression about the lesson you are going to study, whatever may be the subject. Don't just open the book and start reading the lesson. First become mentally ready and be prepared about what you are going to study. Don't just say to yourself, 'Book of history, lesson 12, page 56, 'India's struggle of independence'; and directly open the page and start reading the lesson. No! Open the lesson and see how many pages it has. Are there any photographs? Are there any sub sections? What are the headings of those sub sections? How many questions are there at the end of the lesson? Notice all such things. It may not take more than two minutes. (Rather, it *should* not take more than two minutes!) But it is very helpful. In fact, it is essential.

Have you noticed the first thing any good batsman does, whenever he comes to the ground to start his innings? When he walks to the ground, he never directly takes his position to face the bowler. He first takes a good look around. Where are the fielders placed? What is their body language? How does the mood of umpires look like? What is the mood of the spectators? Every good batsman first gets a feel about all these things by carefully looking around, and then takes his stance and looks towards the bowler. He is then ready for the job!

The same is true here also. When you start studying a lesson, first do the foreseeing part. In fact, even if you want to read a book, do the same thing (except, of course, for novels!). And remember, this should be done within a few minutes.

2) The next step is 'I'.

'I' stands for 'Inquiring'. That means you start reading the lesson by keeping your mind in an 'inquiry' mode. Keep your mind alert, while reading. Let questions occur to you while reading and continue reading to seek their answers. Ability to raise questions while reading is a sign of an alert and inquiring mind. Of course, this is not very easy. As a student, you are always expected to be in the 'answering' mode! Your ability to answer questions in an examination decides your success in that examination. Those students, who enthusiastically raise their hands and give correct answers quickly in the class, are considered bright students. Of course, there is nothing wrong in that. But the ability of students to raise good and pertinent questions is also important, and needs to be developed. If you develop that habit, it will be a great asset to you in your later life as well. So, be receptive to questions that come to your mind while reading. Make conscious efforts to seek questions; and you read further to find their answers.

This is the best way to concentrate on reading. Because, for questions to come to your mind, you have to be mentally active and react to whatever it is that you are reading. You should not be a passive reader. A passive reader reads the words, the sentences; but does not think about what he is reading. An active reader reacts and thinks while reading. Raising questions in your mind; and then trying to find their answers as you read, is the best technique of active reading. (Another technique is 'note taking', about which we will discuss later.) Also, most of the time, there is some underlying central idea discussed in the paragraphs that you are reading (Except for novels and story books). Try to figure out what that idea is.

For example, the central idea in our last two paragraphs is that, while reading, the students must be mentally alert, and active.

3) The third step is 'T'.

'T' is for 'Teaching': It is an effective and a time saving technique. It helps students in many different ways. What you have to do in this technique of studying is the following. **(Para A)**

(We are calling five paragraphs here as 'A', 'B', 'C', 'D', 'E'. The purpose will be clear later.)

While preparing any lesson from a book, stop intermittently after every few minutes; and recite softly orally to yourself, whatever you have read in that time. Thus, while you are studying, stop reading in between. Close the book, and then softly speak out the matter to yourself. Just remembering the main points and key words of the portion you learnt is not enough. Speak out to yourself, as if you are teaching the matter to yourself. As if you were the teacher, and you were the student! You explain the matter to yourself; and you learn the matter from yourself! **(Para B)**

You see, teaching is the best method of learning. When you teach, you really learn! When you try to teach for the first time, you may frequently get stuck. Doesn't matter! If required, you may open the book and refer it wherever you get stuck. Then close the book and continue your teaching. Remember the rule: while you are actually teaching yourself, the book must be closed. Repeat teaching the same matter again the second and the third time. When you do it for the third time, you will be able to do it without looking into the book. **(Para C)**

It is possible that one of your parents or some other elder member of the family is ready to spare her time, and tells you that you can 'teach' her instead of yourself while reading. Such a help from your parents, no doubt, has certain advantages. But, there are disadvantages too. Sparing time as per your schedule of study may not always be possible for that elder. Also, seeking help in this way from someone else may become your necessity while studying; and it may prove to be a hindrance later on in your student life. Your progress in studies will become dependent on the availability of some other person. That is not desirable. **(Para D)**

You see, however attractive they may look, we should not resort to short term solutions. We are looking out for techniques here, which will last you for all your student-years, and also in your later life. So, even if your mother is ready to spare her time for you now, and help you in the technique of 'teach yourself' during your studies, use her help only in the beginning, for a short period of time. Preferably, use this help for a few initial months only, so that you master the technique. After that you should be able to do the part of 'teach yourself' all alone by yourself. The ideal situation is, 'You are the teacher and you are the student.' **(Para E)**

One question could (or should) come to your mind. It is, 'what is meant by 'intermittent', when we say, stop intermittently'? In other words, how often should I stop to 'teach myself'? Is it after, say, every ten minutes? Or, is it after one page of the book? Or, is it at the end of the chapter, or at the end of the lesson? (Do you understand what we are doing here and at many other places in this book? We have said earlier that while reading you must be in the 'inquiring' mode; so that questions occur to you and you continue to read, finding their answers. We are raising those questions for you here, so that you understand the technique. And, of course, we are also providing answers!)

So, the question is, 'what is the meaning of 'intermittent' here'? Now, the answer to this is not simple. Definitely, do not wait until you complete the chapter/lesson, because that would be too heavy or too lengthy for you to recite or to teach. Also, there cannot be a simple rule like 'do it after every one page; or every five minutes' That kind of a rule is too rigid and mechanistic to help you in understanding the subject matter. Doing it after every one or two sentences would be absolutely futile, because that way you cannot understand anything, nor can you teach. So, what is the meaning of 'intermittent'? When do you stop reading intermittently to teach yourself?

The answer is the following. Whenever you feel while reading, that discussion of a central point or a central idea has been covered, you can stop there to teach yourself.

Now, we are sure, you will find this difficult initially. You may wonder, 'how do I decide that the discussion of one point is over? And how do I decide in the first place, what is that central point?' But that precisely is the strength of this technique. You see, your comprehension improves when you start noticing which central point is being discussed at any place in an article, and where it is concluded. The technique we are suggesting, forces students to note both these points. That automatically makes you an active reader. For example, in this chapter we have marked some paragraphs above as 'Para A', 'Para B', 'Para C', 'Para D' and 'Para E'. Now, there is one central point in the paragraphs A, B, C. There is another central point in paragraphs D and E. can you notice and state these central points? (We have given the answer at the end of this chapter. But, don't rush to see that. Try to figure it out first, and then check.)

We do, however, appreciate the fact that for the fresh students, new to this technique, the criterion we have suggested above is not easy. So we give below a simpler rule for beginners. It is not an ideal rule; but would work fine in the beginning. As you become experienced in the technique, you will automatically develop a feel, as to which would be a proper place to stop and teach yourself.

The rule for the beginners is, after around 25 lines, stop at the end of a paragraph, and then recite the matter. That is, there are two conditions: about 25 lines of the book; and then reaching the end of a paragraph.

Now, there are diagrams and figures in a lesson of science and mathematics. Also, there are some mathematical steps. So, while reciting the matter orally, draw those diagrams or write down the mathematical steps in a rough note book. Think how your teacher would have explained the matter to you across the table, while solving your difficulty. You have to use the same method.

Also, after reading it only once, you may not be able to teach yourself. So, you may have to read the part of the lesson two or three times, before you start teaching yourself. In the beginning you will not find it easy to teach yourself. You may get stuck in between, and may have to refer the book very frequently. But, in spite of such difficulties, continue the practice. After a few months you will learn the technique. And once you do that, you will actually start enjoying your studies.

You will also notice that your performance in the examinations has improved beyond your expectations.

What are the advantages of this technique of 'you teach yourself'?

One advantage, of the method is that since, as we mentioned earlier, teaching is the best method of learning rather than rote learning, you will really understand the subject matter. Secondly, normally the aim before you while studying is to prepare for an examination. But the examination may be a few weeks or months away. So, there is no immediate goal in site for you. As a result, your concentration is not at its optimum.

What the technique of 'you teach yourself' does is to introduce an immediate goal, an immediate activity for you, during your studies. That improves your attention. That gives you an immediate motivation. You are more alert while reading the lesson. And, you will experience shortly, that teaching is a creative job. So you start enjoying your studies. Also, while teaching, you develop the skill of putting the matter systematically. This is the most essential skill in writing answer papers in the examination.

The most important point is that this technique in the long run saves your time. Once you master this technique, you complete your studies of any lesson in much less time, and with greater confidence.

(4) Fourth step is 'T' again.

'T' here is for 'Tele-writing'. It means you write down whatever you have studied without looking into book after a gap of time. When you prepare the topic by the above three steps, immediately write down the matter. Again, you may get stuck at some points. Open the book and read that part. Then close the book and write it. You should refer the book as little as possible. But what is important is that every time when you are writing in the notebook, the book must be closed. At no time should the book and the note book both be open. Also writing the same matter after a gap of a few days is very important. (You may revise briefly before you write after a gap.)

This technique of 'Tele-writing' is very important, because our memory fades very fast. Things which we read, study or even experience tend to evaporate quickly. So, train yourself to remember the studied matter after some gap of time. Later in this book, we have explained methods and steps to improve your memory. They will help you in remembering the studied matter, even after a gap of time.

So, the 'strategy' of study consists of three main points. 1) Revise every day what was taught in the class on that day. 2) Have a proper time table and a proper place for study at home. 3) Use the 'FITT' technique for study.

[Answers to questions asked earlier in the chapter: The central point in paragraphs 'A, B and C' is, 'teaching yourself is the best method of learning'. The central point in paragraphs 'D and E' is, 'develop the habit, so that you work out the process of teaching yourself all alone'.]

9

Improve Your Memory.

Psychologists have shown that normally nearly 50% of matter recorded in the brain, is lost in one hour; 65% is lost in a day, and 80% is lost in a month! Do you think, this tendency of human brain to forget things is a disadvantage? No. On the contrary, it is a boon in disguise. If nature had not provided us with this ability of automatically clearing our minds continuously and speedily; our minds would become packed bags within no time, loaded with all and sundry details of our daily lives; and that load would have made us insane! So, it is a good thing that our memory erases out fast!

But there is also a strength that we possess. We can choose and decide things we do not want to forget, and keep them in our memory for a much longer time; and sometimes, even for our life time. One factor which facilitates this process is our field of interest. You also must have experienced this. Things related to the field in which you are interested are automatically committed to your memory. Those of you, for example, who are ardent cricket lovers, easily remember so much of the history of cricket. They can easily quote scores of leading batsmen, and details of any particular cricket match. Similarly, those who are fans of Hindi movies will remember all the Bollywood stuff readily.

Now, all of you also want to remember whatever you study and commit it to memory, so that your performance in examinations improves. Based on the above observation, what can be the prescription? Well, 'be genuinely interested in whatever you are studying'. Quite simple and logical! But that is more easily said than done! To be frank, it is unfair to expect from a student, that he should develop interest in all the subjects being taught. Interest cannot be developed forcibly. It comes spontaneously. A student can have natural interest only in one or two subjects; not all! Some may find the subject of 'history' very interesting; some may find mathematics very interesting. But, of course, a student cannot afford to concentrate only on the subjects of liking, and neglect other subjects.

But, though genuine *liking* may be there only for a few subjects, genuine *desire* has to be there to remember studied portion from all the subjects. Such a genuine desire creates motivation, and that helps you in your studies. And, as a student, you must have a genuine desire to improve your memory. It will be an asset which will give you immense benefits in your student life, and also in your later life. There are some techniques to improve your memory, and we are now going to reveal those techniques to you. Again, there are no short cuts here, but there are some tried and tested methods, and techniques.

The first thing is that understanding of the study material is a must. Rote learning can fail your memory any time. Cramming things in the memory without understanding is not the way to study. Such a method may appear to be successful for students in lower standards; but the result is illusive. It is bound to be short lived. It may, perhaps, help at school level, or higher secondary level; but definitely no further. As a student proceeds to higher and higher standards, the success level of rote learning starts declining; and the method is a sure failure at professional courses, or at higher levels of study. So, the first rule is, 'understand the subject matter, if you want to remember it'.

But, this rule is not always helpful. Because, there are many cases, where you have to just remember details, and there is very little to understand in those details. For example, there are different dates and years of historically important events. You have to remember those dates while studying history. Now, it is true that there are factors, which have affected the way in which history unfolded itself; and the course of history can be logically explained and understood on the basis of those factors. But there is no logic for a particular date and year in which a particular event occurred. Such dates have to be remembered. Spellings of words in English have to be remembered. There are some common patterns, which may help in remembering spellings; but there is no logic there.

This is true, even in case of subjects like science and mathematics (which are supposed to be more 'logical subjects' and are based on pure understanding). Formulae for circumference and area of a circle and volume of a sphere have to be remembered. (You can then understand and hence remember the formulae for area and volume of a cylinder). The names and sequence of colors in a rainbow must be remembered. The chemical notations for elements in Chemistry have to be remembered. So, the point is that, though cramming is not advisable, memorizing certain things while studying has no option. And the techniques, we are presently going to explain, will help you in your memorizing such things.

One useful technique is 'peg' technique. A peg is a small nail hammered into a wall on which a big bag loaded with many things can be suspended. Similarly, we can use some small acronyms, which are easily remembered; and with the help of which we remember many more things. For example, the method of study we described earlier was called the 'FITT Method'. 'FITT' is an acronym, a word formed by taking first letters of four words, 'Foreseeing', 'Inquiring', 'Teaching' and 'Tele-writing'. The word 'FITT' otherwise has no meaning, but in the present context, it has a meaning. You will easily remember this word, and because of that you will remember all the details of the method of study discussed under that heading.

The best example of an acronym, which is known to everyone, is the word 'VIBGYOR'. The word by itself has no meaning. But when you think of it, you immediately remember that there are seven colors in a rainbow, you remember their names and also the sequence in which they appear! Normally, it would have been very difficult to memorize all this information, and would have required a lot of efforts. But the word 'VIBGYOR' has made the job very simple, and almost everyone easily remembers this information. That is the advantage of forming an acronym. That is the strength of the 'peg' technique.

Wherever possible you can try and form acronyms to be used as pegs and suspend a bag containing a lot of information to be remembered. The instant you pronounce the word you will remember all the information. 'Pronounce' is the key word. The acronym formed need not be independently a known, meaningful word. It can be a completely new combination of letters. But it must have a pronunciation.

Sometimes, it is difficult to form an acronym. Then you can form a sentence to remember information. Those of you who are in higher standards, and have studied trigonometry, must have come across a well known sentence, 'all silver tea cups!' This is used to remember that all trigonometric functions are positive in the first quadrant of a co-ordinate system, only 'sines' are positive in the second quadrant, only 'tangents' are positive in the third quadrant, and only 'cosines' are positive in the fourth quadrant. (Those of you who have not studied trigonometry will not understand this. Ignore the details, and remember the point.) The point is that 'peg' is not always a single word. Sometimes, it is a combination of words, or a sentence, which becomes helpful in remembering the information.

But 'peg' method has its limitations also. You cannot use it in every case. For example, spellings of words in English cannot be remembered by the 'peg' method. Or, in higher classes, students have to remember chemical notations for elements, and chemical formulae. (For example, Hydrogen is H_2 and Oxygen is O_2 and water is H_2O). Or, there are poems in your text books of languages. And you have to memorize them. For such things, the method is to recite them again and again, and recite them frequently. 'Frequently' is the key word. Rather than reciting 20 times continuously, it is more effective and time saving, if you recite 10 times on one day, five times after, say, four or five days; and again five times after five days. The chances are that this way you will remember the matter easily, and for a longer time. May be, you can devote one 'period' on two days or three days in a week in your time table 'home-study', for reciting the topics to be memorized. Also, you can write the matter to be memorized on a sheet of paper, and suspend it on some wall of your house, so that you can glance at it, read it frequently every day while moving around in the house. You can change the sheet every week. This appears to be a simple technique, but is extremely effective and time saving.

May be, you can take help of your mother or some other elder in the family in this case for preparing the sheets to be suspended. But, let us be clear. Reciting again and again, and frequently, involves hard work and consumes time. And there is no substitute for it.

However there is good news in this connection. The more you memorize things by reciting, the stronger becomes your memory. The time required for memorizing decreases progressively. Actually, your brain gets trained to memorize things. The sheer reason is 'practice'. An athlete, for example, trains his body for running a long distance without fatigue; or for lifting heavy weights without faltering. How? Simply by regular practice! Similarly, when you practice memorizing things, you increase the memory power of your brain. Some students have a wrong notion, that by memorizing more and more things, the brain is taxed; and its ability to memorize further decreases. This is wrong. By running every day during practice, the capacity of the athlete increases; and not decreases. Same is true here.

Scientists tell us that our brain has enormous potential, and a normal person uses hardly 10% of it in his life. That also includes the memory power of the brain. Actually, today's generation is, in a sense, quite lucky as far as load of memorization is concerned. Many gadgets are available today, which reduce load on memory. Before electronic calculators were available, for example, students had to remember multiplication tables from2 to 30. That is no longer necessary. Computers, and also some applications of mobile phones, can indicate mistakes in spellings when you write them; and even suggest corrections. These devices really reduce the load of memorization on students, and improve their confidence. The requirement of memorizing for studies has definitely reduced in many areas (though not all).

But committing to memory certain things does have its advantages even in today's world. So, make it a point to strengthen your memory. Do train your brain to memorize things quickly. Take efforts for that. And do it in your student days. Actually, what you can do is to memorize some classic book like 'Bhagvad Geeta', or Rabindranaath Tagore's Nobel Prize winning book of poems 'Geetanjali', or the 'Shero-Shayari' of Urdu language. This will make you an impressive conversationalist in any group. And it will also improve your memory. Later on you will find, that a strong memory, developed consciously during student days, is a million dollar asset even in the days of computers and mobiles and calculators!

10

Speed Reading.

Reading is the basic activity for study. In fact 'reading' is a word used for 'studying' in many languages, including English. In the present age of technology, information dissemination can take place by various different modes. It could be regular film strips, animation films, power point presentations or recorded lectures. All these methods have their advantages. But ultimately, they help the process of reading. Also, when you want to understand a subject, a theory or a technique, there is no substitute for reading.

Not only for studies; reading is also a good recreation activity. Reading enriches your life. Reading good books opens up windows which bring you new knowledge, new experiences, new sensitivities. Reading has not become obsolete in the age of computers and internet. It is a misconception that the importance of reading has declined in the present age. The reality is quite the opposite.

Today the internet, through its search engines like Google, literally pours information before you on any topic of your interest within a fraction of a second. Internet, perhaps, has little role to play in your regular studies. But, if you have done any project as a co-curricular activity, you must have used the internet. In any case, it is going to be an essential part of your activities in higher studies, and later on in your professional life. Though some material available on the net is in the form of films, videos and photographs; most of it is reading material.

So reading has actually become a key part of our lives in the modern world; and speed reading has become an important skill that everyone must possess. We give below a few tips for speed reading that will help you as students. There are some more tips, which will be useful to you in your later life, when you enter a job or a profession. But those tips are not useful to you as students. So, in order to avoid confusion we confine ourselves to giving tips useful for students.

First, try to understand how we read. We know that the written matter is composed of words, and the words are composed of letters. But when we read we read the words and not the letters. For example, when you read the word 'apple' you notice the entire word together, all five letters of it. Only then can you understand the word, its meaning. If you had read each letter separately like 'a—p—p—l—e', it would have been difficult for you to understand what the word was. You would have finally understood the word, but after a comparatively longer time. When you read all the five letters together, you quickly understand the word 'apple'. The ability to read basically comes from the ability to pick up all the letters in a word together.

The ability to read faster comes through just one step ahead of this. It is the ability to pick up a group of words, or a phrase together. While we are reading, our eyes move from left to right along the line. But the movement is 'stop-go-stop-go' type. We stop for a fraction of a second and pick up a phrase or a group of words; then move forward along the line to the next 'stop'. When we stop for a fraction of a second, we pick up at least three words together. The eyes are fixated at one particular word; but human brain has this ability to pick up at least one word before and one word after the word on which the eyes are fixated. Thus we pick up at least three words together. Actually, the fast readers pick up two words from either side of the central word. But that is almost the limit. Picking up more than five words together is difficult; almost impossible.

After reaching the end of the line, our eyes come back fast to the beginning of the next line. But they fixate on the second or third word of the line and start moving in the 'stop-go' pattern on the next line.

You must be saying to yourself, 'this theory about reading is fine. It is interesting as well. But I want practical tips to read faster. If I want to learn swimming, what is the use of knowing Archimedes's principle of buoyancy, and Newton's third law of motion (which explain how we swim)? Well, we just gave a brief idea about the basics of the process of reading. Actually, the connection between language and knowledge is a vast and complex subject (and interesting too). The basic point is that the ability to use language and a mastery over reading and writing are essential features of acquiring and generating knowledge. So, in today's world, one who reads survives; and one who reads faster succeeds!

Therefore, the real question is how to read fast? Well, you start by first checking your present speed of reading. Clock the timing for reading three or four pages of a book. (Of course, don't pick up the book, which you have already read earlier. Or, don't pick up a book on some difficult technical subject.) Then find the average number of words per page. 250 words per minute (wpm) is an average speed of reading. It can easily be increased up to 300 to 350 wpm, i.e. an increase of 20% to 40% in the speed; which amounts to so much of time saving. This difference is huge! And don't try to be over ambitious in this matter. If you increase your reading speed by 20% or so, you should be happy; and if you increase it by say 40%, you should be more than happy!

Also, the speed is dependent on the topic you are reading and the purpose for which you are reading. Technical matters and complex discussions would take more time. Also, the familiarity with the subject makes a difference. A lawyer, for example, would read a legal document very fast, whereas a layman would take a longer time. The above range of 250 wpm to 350 wpm is for general reading; and care must be exercised in applying it to technical or completely unfamiliar subjects.

A good 'phrase sense' is a must for speed reading, because when we read, we pick up phrases (i.e. meaningful group of words) rather than individual words. See the following sentence.

'The art of good reading is composed of a small amount of information and a tremendous amount of practice.'

Now, we split it into meaningful phrases '/ The art of good reading/ is composed of/ a small amount of information/ and a tremendous amount of practice/.'

There are 19 words, but 4 phrases. Developing this 'phrase sense' is crucial to speed reading. It comes by having good understanding of the language. And this, in turn, comes from reading extensively in that language, and also from practice of using that language for writing and speaking. So, for speed reading one simple thing which you must do is to read regularly as an exercise in fast reading. That reading should be in addition to your text book reading. It is not routine reading, it is reading with an intention to improve speed of reading. Understand the '*do and don't*' of speed reading. Certain things are to be avoided; and certain things are to be followed sincerely.

The first thing to avoid is reading out the matter loudly. Even a movement of your lips as you read silently (sub-vocalizing) is not allowed. It is an absolute 'no-no' for speed reading. Reading should be a completely mental activity, and no physical movement should be involved (except that of your eyes). Learn to read silently and with full mental concentration.

Also, try to avoid going back to the words you just read. This may become necessary occasionally, and perhaps more so while reading technical subjects. So, we don't put it into an absolute 'no-no' category. But keep it to the minimum. You see, some readers develop a habit of constantly going back to the earlier matter while reading ahead. Such a habit is bad. It does not improve your comprehension of the reading material, and reduces speed. Actually, it is a question of concentrating on the activity of reading. Lack of concentration forces you to go back to the words just read. You may move your finger just below the line as you read. This helps in concentrating on the reading matter, and also helps in maintaining your speed of reading.

Also, ensure that there is no problem in your eye-sight. With a defective eye-sight, there is frequent watering of eyes, or aching of eyes even when you read for just about fifteen-twenty minutes. If there is any such problem, you should get your eye sight checked by a specialist. If you are avoiding wearing spectacles, when actually they are advised by the specialist, then you should reconsider your decision. In case you are wearing spectacles, then regularly check the number of your glasses and change the glasses, if necessary. Avoid straining your eyes by seeing TV for a long time; and that too from a close distance.

Now, the question is about the daily practice of speed reading. As mentioned earlier, for this you should read matter apart from your text books. (As your reading speed increases, it will also help in reading study material. But don't experiment on speed reading with the study material.) You may wonder, 'but, how can I do it? Now you want me to take out additional time to practice speed reading. Where do I get that time from? I am so busy throughout the day, that it is difficult for me to find time for this additional activity.' You are right! Availability of time is the key factor. But that is what time management is all about. And that is what we are basically talking about throughout.

So, you can practice speed reading daily without taking out extra time for that. How? Well, remember, we told you that reading news paper every day is advisable; in fact, essential. Now, just decide that you would read it daily; and that you would practice fast reading there. Just increase your speed slightly above your comfort level. Don't be too ambitious, otherwise you may be simply gliding your eyes on the matter, without understanding what you are reading. That is a complete failure of the project. So, you should read fast, and you should absorb the material.

News papers are particularly suited for speed reading. Why? Not because, even if you miss some details while reading a news, it makes no big difference to you; but because the news papers are printed in a different manner than other printed material. The news papers are printed in columns, where each column has four to five words. We told you that the trick of fast reading is to fixate your eyes at the central word and to pick up three to five words together. (Three words is normal pattern, and easily possible. Five is more than good. Don't try to be more ambitious!) You can almost move your eyes vertically down while speed reading a news paper column. Also, when you try this initially, you are conscious of what you are doing. That will distract your concentration, and slightly reduce your speed. Don't worry too much about it. Very soon you will learn the trick and your speed will increase.

If you are clear about the purpose for which you are reading the book (or any other reading material) that improves the speed of reading. As far as your study material is concerned, you have to read carefully every word, and should note every point. But, if you are doing extra reading, then first see the general nature of the book by skimming through it (except novels and story books!). You will know what is to be expected by reading the book. If you have some specific questions in mind, and are trying to search answers to them, that will increase your speed.

Sometimes there is a 'comprehension test' in an examination in the question papers of languages. An unseen passage is given for the students to read, and then there are some questions below, answers to which are to be searched in the passage. And, obviously, this has to be completed as fast as possible.

Now, normally a student reads the passage first and questions later and then goes back to the passage again to search answers. But, first glance through the passage quickly just to understand what the topic is (just like 'fore seeing'). Then read the questions first, and then re-read the passage. The comprehension is always faster. Because by reading questions first, you know what the passage is about; and while reading the passage you know what you are looking for. By this method, you may save only a few minutes for attempting the question on comprehension. But those are crucial few minutes in an examination.

So, the point is, it is possible to increase your speed of reading. Continuous efforts of a few months would give you that skill. It is a matter of practice and knowing the technique. But avoid experimenting speed reading on your text books. Develop the skill independently. It will eventually help you in your studies also.

11

Taking Notes in Class.

You should learn the technique of taking notes in the class, while listening to the teacher. There are two points that need discussion in this connection.

The first point is that whether taking notes in the class diverts the attention of students from listening to the teacher. Actually, this is a misconception. It is, no doubt, true that you must fully concentrate on what the teacher is teaching. You must become a good listener. This habit will help you in your student days; and it will also be an asset to you in your later life. All successful people are good listeners. They always listen with full attention. You may wonder then, why taking notes in the class, simultaneously while listening to the teacher is being advised here? Wouldn't that divide the attention of students into two tasks, listening and writing? Wouldn't that affect their concentration?

Well, the reality is just the opposite. Taking notes simultaneously while listening actually helps students to concentrate! Ability to concentrate on a task is not easy. It is especially difficult to concentrate over a long time. The human mind is very difficult to control. When you sit quiet and continue to listen to the teacher, chances are that your mind would slowly start drifting towards some different topic, and you would never realize how and when the process started. This happens particularly when the subject is not of your liking, and when the teacher is not a good speaker. (And all good teachers are not necessarily good speakers!) You realize only after some time that your mind has drifted, and your concentration is lost. You lose the link of the subject, and that makes it more difficult to concentrate again. This is such a common phenomenon that, no doubt, you have experienced it so often.

What is the remedy then? How to prevent the drifting of mind, the loss of attention in a class?

Taking notes while listening is the answer. The first thing is that you are then involved in a physical activity. If your mind drifts, your hand will stop automatically, and you would immediately notice it. You can then force back your attention to the job at hand.

But more important than physical activity is the mental activity in which you are involved. The technique of taking notes simultaneously while listening is to jot down only the important points and words. So, you naturally need to concentrate more on listening to what is being spoken, than you would otherwise. You have to continuously distinguish between the main points and the accompanying explanatory discussion. And all this has to be done 'on line', while you continue to listen. No extra time for that. This is a challenging job demanding much greater focused attention.

The skill in taking notes lies in quickly grasping the main points and important words in whatever you are listening. Remember, only the key words are to be jotted down, not full sentences. For example, suppose instead of reading, you were listening to a lecture on 'techniques of taking notes'. What words from the above paragraphs in this chapter, would you have noted down? (Go back to these paragraphs, and try this as an exercise. We are giving a list at the end of this chapter for comparison. We may mention here that while the four paragraphs contain 461 words, the note contains only 50 words; and they are sufficient to indicate all the important points.)

But this jotting of the key words 'on line' is half the job. Later you have to work on them and complete the 'notes' with full sentences and with 'filling in the blanks'. The jotted down words are like 'pegs' described earlier in the section on memory improvement. Using those clues, you can recollect whatever was discussed during the lecture and prepare full notes. This should be done afterwards, but as early as possible.

There is one more point here that needs some discussion.

These days, notes on virtually all subjects are available in the market or on net. Many coaching classes also provide notes. You may feel, if readymade notes are available, why not use them? Would it not save much precious time? You are right in a sense. Readymade notes are time saving and are professionally prepared. No harm in using them. No harm in taking whatever help that is available around; provided it helps you in your studies and in your personality development. The question then is, why you should undertake the exercise, and spend time and energy in preparing your own notes.

Well, we will tell you why you should prepare your own notes, and also how to save time using the readymade notes.

Now, our suggestion is that you must do your part of jotting down of the important points and words in the class yourself. Do not avoid it. This, as we said earlier, is an 'on line' job and does not require any extra time. You may then skip the next part. That is, instead of preparing full notes from your jotted down words, what you can do is to compare readymade notes of your choice with the jotted down words. You can, thus, check whether you had covered all the points. Also, occasionally, you may add to the readymade notes from the words you jotted down in the class. This would help develop in you a most crucial skill, namely of noting important words and points, while listening to any lecture and presentation. That skill is of utmost importance in higher levels of education; and in any professional career.

Remember, no one is going to give you readymade notes as you rise to higher levels in life. You have to prepare your own notes. And you must know the required technique for the purpose.

(Answer to the exercise given in the chapter.) Notes on the the paragraphs:

notes taking—diverts attention?—good listeners—all leaders—asset—divides attention?—no—mind diverts—is realized late—loss of continuity—normal experience—answer—note taking—physical activity—if stops—loss of concentration noticed—Mental activity—more important—note main points—important words—jot words—on line activity—no extra time.

12

Time Management during Exam Time.

You will surely agree that the most crucial time in a student's life is exam time. Whether one likes it or not, one's success as a student is always judged by performance in examinations. Not everyone can get the first rank or a distinction in an examination. But it is legitimate to expect that every one of you is able to do your best in your exams and should score the maximum possible marks or the highest possible grade.

Have you realized, however, that what is tested in an exam is not only your knowledge and understanding of the subject matter, but also your skills in time management? All examinations, from primary school to high school to undergraduate college levels to the higher level of professional courses have this common characteristic. They test time management skills of candidates. For spectacular success in any examination, there must be a thorough preparation of subject matter; and, equally and perhaps more important, a mastery over 'Exam Technique'. And what is this 'Exam Technique'? It is nothing but the technique of time management during an examination.

This connection between an examination and time management is obvious during the examination, when candidates are actually engaged in solving question papers. But there is something more to this. The connection is equally crucial a month before the scheduled date of examination; and it is more so on the day just prior to the date of the paper. We will systematically explore these aspects of time management before and during the exam time; and will give you some useful tips.

There are two types of examinations that students face today in our education system. Some are 'big examinations', and some are 'small examinations'. 'Big Examinations' are 'semester end exams' (or 'terminal exams'), or 'annual exams' or 'Board or University exams'. Also there are 'entrance exams' for those, who are at the stage of joining professional courses. The so called 'small exams' are 'weekly tests' or 'quizzes' conducted regularly throughout the year in your school or college. A word of caution here, before we proceed further! Let not the nomenclature 'Big' and 'Small' mislead you into thinking that the former are important examinations and the later unimportant. No, absolutely not! The portion for a 'weekly test' or 'quiz' is comparatively small, hence the name 'small'. On the other hand, the portion for 'big examinations' is large. But both should be treated as of equal importance.

You see, a one day match in cricket lasts just for one day. A test match is of five days' duration. But no cricketer would consider one day match to be of less importance. No one would take it lightly. Everyone would try to give his best performance in a test match, as also in a one day match. What differs is the technique. It is a well known fact that the technique of batting or bowling is different in a one day match, from that in a test match. Similarly, both the 'big' and 'small' examinations are of equal importance. What differs is the technique, the technique of time management.

A proper time management reduces exam related tension or stress. Stress is bad and counter-productive. It reduces your energy level; and it diminishes your capacity to concentrate on the job at hand. You must always take every examination seriously; but ideally with no tension. That may not be possible in reality. It is unlikely that you would have no tension related to an examination; but what you can do is to keep it under control. Learning the techniques of time management during exam time is the best way to do that.

Proper revision is the key to success in any exam. When you are about to face a 'big exam', your revision time should start one month before. You should plan your studies, so that a clear one month period is left for revision. No preparation of any new chapter should be left for that last month. You may get your doubts and difficulties cleared if there are any from your teachers; but no fresh reading and preparation in the last month, only the revision. You should devote more time for studies in that last month, and prepare a separate timetable of revision.

Revise every subject at least twice. The first revision should be thorough and in detail. What exactly is to be revised depends upon the subject. We are giving below some guide lines for different subjects, and then will tell you a few general strategies useful for all subjects.

As far as language subjects are concerned, read all the lessons and poems from your text book carefully. Also, carefully go through questions given at the end of each lesson and poem in your text book, and their answers written in your notebook.

Read essays that you have written during the course of the year. If you have some book of essays with you, read those essays also. In case of English language, go through spellings of difficult words.

For science subjects, revising diagrams and derivations is very important. Do not merely see the diagrams in the text books. Draw those diagrams in rough, so that you recollect all the essential points in the diagram. Practice labeling of the diagrams. Similarly, write mathematical steps of derivation in rough, so that you recollect them. (Only reading mathematical steps from a text book is not enough.) Formulas in physics and chemistry should be read carefully, and important ones should again be written in rough to make sure you remember them.

While revising mathematics, formulas and their applications are important. Write the formulas in rough to make sure you remember them. Derivations of formulas must also be revised carefully by writing them out in rough. Read the solved problems in the text book carefully. Also, you may read some typical and difficult problems as solved in your notebook. While doing so, see that you understand each step of the solution.

Then there are subjects of social sciences. Here again read the lessons carefully. In history, put the sequence of events and their corresponding years together in your notebook. Read them frequently. In geography, pay attention to maps and the important information contained in them.

These were some specific instructions for revising some specific subjects. Given below are some general instructions.

Revision is a skilled job, and you must understand and develop that skill. The first point you must realize is that revision is the most important factor deciding your success in the examination. The preparation for revision should actually start with the regular studies from the beginning of the year.

The notes you prepare for every topic should contain all the important points, formulas and words. Important words should be underlined. You must make it a practice to prepare charts of important formulas, definitions and the short words you have coined, as described earlier in describing 'peg method' for techniques to improve memory. The charts should be displayed turn-by-turn on the walls of your home during the month of revision. Put three charts on the walls at a time. You will automatically look at them, while moving around in the home. After three days remove them and put some other charts. Keep on doing this during your month of revision.

Just as you read your notes and text books during revision, what is equally important is to read questions on the portion you are revising. This fact is not normally realized by many students. Read the questions from the text book, the questions asked on that chapter in the earlier question papers, as also questions from a 'question bank', if it is available. Reading questions gives you a proper perspective. Your mind is automatically concentrated on answers to those questions, while you are revising. That makes your efforts more focused and rewarding.

As stated earlier, there must be two revisions of every subject. The first one is thorough, and the second one can be faster. Give about three to four weeks for the first revision, and only about a week to the second revision. Here, you go through the notes and text books quickly. No need to read them again word by word. Have a quick glance. Look at the spellings, formulas, diagrams, maps, your charts, etc. No need to look at questions during the second revision. The second revision is just to consolidate what you have done during the first revision. It is supposed to be quicker, but it is also important and necessary, because it helps you to retain whatever you had studied and revised.

Then there is 'last minute revision' on the day before the paper of any particular subject. This should again be quick and efficient. Just glance through the notes and text book and your charts. Sit quietly, close your eyes and try to recollect the subject matter. Do all this without any hurry and haste. Be careful that you do not develop any tension in your mind during this last minute revision. It is actually meant to be a confidence booster for you, and for putting your mind in the exam mode.

All the above tips are for the 'big exams'. As far as 'small exams' are concerned, the revision is still important, but the technique is different. The portion for small exams is quite limited and, therefore, the time for revision should also be small. Just devote one day prior to the exam for your first and second revisions as explained above. The last minute revision may be done in ten to fifteen minutes on the day of the paper. Even if more time is available, make it a point that you do not take more than a day for the first two revisions, and more than fifteen minutes for the last minute revision.

These kinds of 'small' examinations are not over, even after you come out of school and college. Every person has to face exam. - like situations in later life, whatever career he/she chooses. There may be some important meeting that you have to address, some presentation to be made, some project to be defended, some crucial negotiations to be done, and so on. All these are exam - like situations in real life. People, who face these situations without tension and perform well are always successful in their lives. For giving the best performance, preparation of what you are going to say, and how you are going to put it is very crucial; and the 'last minute revision' of those points makes a big positive difference. Therefore, it is not only for your success in an examination that you should develop the skill of a quick and efficient revision, it is for your success in later life too.

The real test of time management is, however, on the 'Dee Day', the day of the paper; and that too during the time when you are solving the paper. You have to complete the paper in a specific time of, say, two or three hours. Often students complain that the question paper was easy, but lengthy. They knew answers to all the questions, but the time was insufficient. They could not complete the paper in time. This is the most unfortunate thing to happen in a student's life. All the time spent on study and revision and preparation of exam could yield no result, because the time management during the examination was faulty. Very sad! So, you must be careful about time management during the examination.

For this, what you should do is to assess the time available per question, and decide your speed accordingly. Let us say, there is a paper of two hours' duration and five questions are to be answered. Then the time per question works out to be 22 minutes. For convenience take it as 20 minutes per question. So you have 100 minutes to write the answers and 20 minutes to read the question paper, and to check the answer paper at the end.

Now while writing the answer paper, do keep a watch on the time and see that every question is completed in approximately 20 minutes. It is like the strategy of the side batting second in a one day match. They know the target, and they know the number of overs available. But the strategy is to convert the target into runs per over, and to maintain that scoring rate. The actual run rate can become slower in some overs, but it can be adjusted later since they know the required run rate per over. Similarly, rather than saying 'one paper and two hours', better look at it as 'five questions and two hours' or better still 'twenty minutes per question'.

The remainder of the twenty minutes in the above calculation during those two hours must be used skillfully, because every minute during an examination is valuable, and should be used profitably. One important activity for which this time can be used is reading the question paper. Remember, the questions in the paper must be read carefully. Saving time by reading questions hurriedly during an examination is a bad strategy of time management and can prove to be very costly. So, read questions carefully, even if it means spending a little more time for that activity.

If time is available at the end of the paper, then check your answer paper. But, the question is, 'what is to be checked in your answer paper'? That should be planned carefully in advance. Do not start by reading your answers word by word. First check that you have solved all the required questions. If there are options in the question paper, then check that you have chosen the options correctly. Then check that you have written the correct question number before starting every answer. If you are writing answer to question 1(A), but just mention 'Q.1' before starting the answer, then the examiner is justified in giving zero marks, even if the answer is correct; because the examiner is not supposed to read the answer and locate the question to which it belongs and then give the marks! So first check that all the required questions are solved, and then check that the question numbers are written correctly.

What you check further depends on the nature of the subject. If there are diagrams in the answers, then check the diagrams. See that proper labeling is done. If there are sums, then check the steps of the sum. Ensure that no silly mistakes have been committed while solving. If it is a physics or chemistry paper, then check that proper units have been written in the answers of the sum.

If the subject is such that there are no diagrams or sums, and if time is left then you can start reading the answers word by word. But do one thing. While reading, underline the important words in the answers. This will help you indirectly. It will be a good time management for the examiner! You see, the examiner, who is going to assess your paper later, would like to complete her job as fast as possible, without compromising the quality of work. If important words in the answers are underlined, the work of the examiner becomes easier and faster. The examiner is naturally pleased with such a student, and would tend to give a mark or two more, if there is a possibility. (However, give priority to completing the paper first; and then underline important words if time is available.)

The basic point is that every minute of those two hours, when you are solving an examination paper is important. A good time management during examination means completing the paper in time without hurry and tension; and utilizing profitably the extra time if it is available, for which the strategy must be planned in advance. We have given tips above with the same purpose.

The best way to master the technique of time management during examinations is to write mock examinations. You can find some earlier papers of the examination for which you are preparing. Or, you can request your teacher to set a 'practice paper' of that examination. Also, some schemes of 'test series' are available in the market, for board examinations and for certain subjects. Take advantage of such series if possible. Write a few practice papers in the 'exam mode' where you will solve the paper without disturbance, without referring to books and notebooks, and in the specified time limit. This has immense advantages.

Finally, we talk about the time management during the 'objective type' of question papers. In many entrance examinations of professional courses today, the question papers are of objective type. Here the candidates have to just pick up the right answer to a question from the choices (normally four) given. There is no need to draw diagrams or write descriptive answers. You only need to put a tick mark on the correct answer. In this sense such examinations are simple for the candidates. But actually they are a real test of the time management skills of candidates. This is because a large number of questions have to be attempted in a limited time. Typically there are 100 questions in 100 minutes; i.e. one question per minute! That, sure, is very fast! Also, the questions are such that they test analytical ability of the candidate. Sometimes very specific information in the subject matter is asked, which requires a quick ability to recollect.

Time management for such type of papers is very crucial and not easy to teach. However, there are two or three important tips. The first is that a thorough preparation of subject matter, and a practice of solving objective type of papers is a must. Secondly, since a large number of questions are to be read here and answers are required to be given fast, you may tend to read questions in a hurry to save time. But that is absolutely wrong here. So read every question with full concentration and care. The third tip is that all four options are also to be read carefully. Actually, if you first read the options given, and then read the question preceding them, it would help. It would give you a hint on what to concentrate on while reading the question and save some time. It is a useful tip. Try it in your practice papers first.

And remember, concentration is the key while solving objective type of question papers. Do not let anything distract your attention while solving these papers.

If you follow these tips for time management during exam time, you would definitely improve your performance beyond your expectation. We wish you all the best.

13

Positive Thinking.

The three of them, the daughter, her father and mother sat there across the table facing the Principal. The mother was almost in tears, and could start crying any minute. The father was quiet, but looked sad and depressed. The daughter was trying to control her tears; but defying her efforts some tears did roll down her cheeks. There was gloom in the cabin, the cabin of the Principal of a reputed college in the city.

It was only a year back, the Principal remembered, the same family had sat in the same cabin, with their faces beaming with smiles. The girl had secured admission to the college on merit; and the three of them had come to see him, to make a courtesy call, like many parents did after admission. The parents were happy and spoke with evident pride about their daughter, how she was a good and hard-working student in her studies; and how she also excelled in elocution and debates, and had won many prizes in inter-school competitions. The beautiful young girl sat there contented and confident. Her glowing eyes could barely hide the fact that she was dreaming of a big and bright future ahead of her. The Principal too happily shared their joy.

And now the picture was exactly the opposite. The scene could not have been more different. What had happened? Well, the young girl had not done well at all in her first year of college. She had barely scraped through her examinations and had not shown any notable performance in extra-curricular activities. What was worse, her confidence had vanished and her eyes seemed empty, devoid of any dreams.

'We do not know what has happened to her, but she is completely lost. She is unusually quiet and rarely speaks to anyone. She tries to be aloof and withdrawn,' her mother spoke in a quivering voice. 'She no longer is interested in any activity at home or outside. Her health too is on the decline.'

'We have told her', continued the father, 'that even if she did not score good percentage this year, it would not matter. That could be made up later. But what we want is our cheerful little daughter back. Why is she like this now? What has gone wrong?' He spoke so feebly, his last question was barely audible.

Having seen so many students pass through the college for many years, the Principal thought he knew just what was wrong, and what the remedy was. He reassured the parents, talked to the girl for some time, and gave her some simple advice to follow. When they left, the parents were a little more assured, yet not convinced enough that the advice given by the Principal would work. The girl continued to seem confused and unsure about herself. Even the Principal was not quite certain what the outcome of his advice was likely to be.

But, apparently she did follow the advice. The young girl was soon back to her normal self, scored good marks in her next examination, and later won many prizes in elocution competitions for the college, and more importantly her self-confidence was restored.

What had gone wrong? What advice did the Principal give her?

Well, it was essentially what Mr. Lee had told Mr. Schewab, Chairman of Bthlehem Steel Company, a century ago. (We have told you that story earlier.) In short, what the Principal advised her was that she follow the simple technique of time management, explained to you in detail in this book.

What had happened to the girl was not uncommon. You see, what happens is that when you step into a new college environment from the earlier school environment, you step into a much wider circle. (From there, you step into the still much bigger open world outside.) Children are more protected in a school environment. Also, they are guided at every step by their parents and teachers in the school. Colleges are different. There is an air of freedom and personal autonomy in a college. Further, most students suddenly feel that they are grown up now, and do not like their parents and teachers breathing down their neck all the time.

But, under such circumstances, students who do not know how to manage their own affairs with available time, find themselves at a loss. They get confused and tensed up as so many things have to be done in a day; and they do not know how to plan their day. Then they start losing confidence. Some cases eventually become acute (like the one of this young girl) and are serious enough to be of concern to parents and others; some are not so noticeable. But the effects of confusion and tension are there.

The best way to avoid such a situation would be to learn systematically the technique of time management; and to learn it as early as possible. This is why this book is written. Remember, the pressures of work and deadlines do catch up with everyone, as we move ahead in life. When that happens, it does create a crisis of self-confidence, that disturbs one's mental peace. The best way is to remain prepared for that day from an early stage of life. That is why understanding and practicing the techniques of time management in your student days is so important.

There is one more angle to this story. There is one more thing that the Principal told that young girl, which we want to share with you. It is about the way you think.

You are what you think! Your thoughts shape your personality. Your thoughts decide your destiny. It is a subject, discussed at great length by philosophers. It is a subject, discussed in all religious scriptures.

What you think is the most important thing of your life. Do you know what a prayer in Sanskrit says?

It says, 'For destroying the thoughts of enmity.'

It does not say, 'For destroying the enemy.'

It does not pray for the destruction of enemy, but for the destruction of the *thoughts* of enmity.

The wise men of the past had long realized that thoughts determine the behavior of a person. If the mind is filled with thoughts of enmity, the person behaves like an enemy. If those thoughts are destroyed, he becomes a friend. Just as the outcome you see on the screen of a computer is really determined by the steps written in its program, the behavior of a person is determined by what kind of thoughts the person harbors in his or her head. If a computer is giving faulty results, the fault lies in the program, and the program has to be corrected. Similarly, if a person behaves in a faulty manner, the fault lies in his thoughts; and that has to be corrected.

And this was the other thing, which the Principal told bright young girl in our story. Actually, her problem basically was not very serious. Scoring low marks in an exam, or not being able to perform well in a few competitions in a year is not a very serious matter. It became serious, because as a result of this, she started thinking in a wrong way. But, unlike a computer, human beings have this special ability that they can correct their own 'programs'; i. e. their 'thinking process'. Sometimes it is not easy; it requires strong will and determination, but it is always possible. So it was pointed out to the girl what was wrong in her thinking process, and what change she needed to make. She followed the advice and benefitted immensely.

What was the fault that had crept in her thinking process? You must understand this because it can happen to anyone, to you as well. As a result of a few setbacks she started thinking in a negative manner. She let her confidence be lost, and started feeling convinced, that she was a loser. She feared that her good days were over in the school; and however hard she might try, she would not be able to get the same success. Such negative thoughts are extremely harmful to our personality and well being, but many of us are victims of this negative thinking. Nearly all mental problems of a person, from worry, fear and depression, can be traced to the habit of negative thinking. Most of the failures in life have their roots in the lack of positive thinking.

So, what and how you think is the most crucial single factor in your life. You can convert difficulties into opportunities and adversities into challenges just by changing how you think. This is something which is entirely in your control, because no one else in this world, however powerful, can regulate your thoughts. Only you have that power. You must have determination to use that power; and should know what kind of thoughts you should entertain.

You see, you must always think of your strengths and your successes. You must always think positive. You must always believe that you have the capacity to work hard, and that you will succeed. You must believe that you have the determination to overcome any shortcomings and hurdles which might impede your progress. Keep on repeating to yourself, 'I have a strong will power. I will put in all my efforts, and I will succeed.' Always think of being successful, of having all the good qualities in your personality that you desire. When you are learning the techniques of time management, always have a firm belief that you have the capacity to master these techniques; and are determined to master them and that success is guaranteed for you. This is one common thing among all happy, confident and successful people. They always think positive.

But, a word of caution here is necessary.

There is a distinction between positive thinking and wishful thinking. For example, you cannot win a big lottery by positive thinking! You may dream intensely about winning it, but that is wishful thinking. Positive thinking is certainly about your being successful, but first it should have a component of your strong will power, then your determined efforts, and consistent hard work. It is then that the success follows positive thinking.

Another point. It is natural that a person is full of positive thoughts, when, as is said, 'the times are good', when everything is fine and as per expectations, and success is achieved. The real testing time is when things do not go as per expectations, and when the desired success is not achieved. It is at such times that one may become a victim of negative thinking (as did the young girl in our story). Such times are bound to come in everyone's life. It is for such times that one must develop a strong attitude of positive thinking.

There are some tried and tested techniques for this. Again, they are simple, and let not the simplicity deceive you. Here is one, which is the simplest to practice, and yields the best results.

Every night, just when you go to bed lie straight first, facing the ceiling. Then let your eyes be closed, and body be relaxed completely. Feel your body is relaxing progressively. You should feel that your legs are relaxing————relaxing————relaxed. They have gone completely limp. There is no tension in them. Then the mussels in your stomach are relaxed. Then your arms, your shoulders are relaxed. Your eyes are relaxed. You are completely relaxed. There is no tension in any part of the body. Then softly speak to yourself, 'I am always happy. I am always very happy. I have a strong will power. I have a very strong will power. I put in my full efforts in every work that I undertake, and I always do the best. I always finally succeed. I am always successful in practicing time management. The God always helps me. I am happy, and now I will sleep peacefully.' (Those who do not believe in God may drop that sentence and say, 'my subconscious always helps me'.) After repeating for five times, you may change your position of lying straight, facing the ceiling. You may take any other comfortable position for sleeping; but keep on repeating the lines until you fall asleep. Do this regularly every day; and experience the wonder. You will always have positive thinking, and a positive attitude towards your life.

14

Ready!–––Steady!–––Go!

This is the last page of this book.

It was a pleasure sharing our ideas with you on the crucial subject of 'Time Management'

We hope, indeed we are sure; you too enjoyed reading the book with interest and attention.

You will soon find that this book has changed your thinking and attitude forever.

We tried in this book to give you some very useful tips.

We shared with you some very useful techniques.

There will be immense benefits, if you follow these tips and techniques.

Also, we advise you to read the book frequently for continued best outcomes.

Managing time means managing your own life.

There is no power greater than the power to manage your own life.

You have that power now.

You are set on the path of a successful and enriched life.

You can reap the benefits in your present phase- the student phase-, and also in your later life.

Your life will change as never before; and the change is for the better.

The only condition is that you practice what you have read.

So start on this path of success and happiness.

Start from *today*.

All the Best!

Ready————Steady————Go!

www.ingramcontent.com/pod-product-compliance
Lightning Source LLC
Chambersburg PA
CBHW022020170526
45157CB00003B/1306